Desserts
from the Garden

Janet Ballantyne

GARDEN WAY PUBLISHING
Pownal, Vermont 05261

Acknowledgments

I would like to thank all the people who so eagerly ate the desserts I tested for this book. Special thanks go to Kirk Trabant for her assistance in testing recipes, to my editor, Andrea Chesman, and to Ann Aspell and Andrea Gray for the beautiful book design.

Illustrations by Elayne Sears

Copyright 1983 by Storey Communications, Inc.

The name Garden Way Publishing is licensed to Storey Communications, Inc.
by Garden Way, Inc.

Printed in the United States.

Printing (last digit): 10 9 8 7 6 5 4 3 2

Library of Congress Cataloging in Publication Data

Ballantyne, Janet, 1952-
    Desserts from the garden.

    Includes index.
    1. Desserts.   2. Cookery (Fruit)   3. Cookery
(Vegetables)   I. Title.
TX773.B27   1983   641.8′6   83-1566
ISBN 0-88266-322-4

Contents

Preface

I have a sweet tooth and I love desserts. Making desserts from the garden is my way of transforming wonderful vegetables into desserts that include vitamins, minerals, and fiber. Do these desserts taste healthy? Never. They taste delicious! Just try the Zucchini Chocolate Crinkles, the Carrot Custard Pie, or the Beet Cheesecake.

Beet cheesecake? Yes, that is a little far-fetched (and humorous). But the second reason I embarked on this cookbook is that I get alot of satisfaction from cooking home-grown produce. The satisfaction is triple with a meal made from soup to dessert with fresh fruits and vegetables from the garden.

Many of the recipes were developed to make use of those garden vegetables that always produce a surplus. There are many recipes here for green tomatoes and summer squash. If you want even more recipes, look for my *Red and Green Tomato Cookbook* from Garden Way and *Garden Way's Zucchini Cookbook* by Marynor Jordan and Nancy Ralston.

Gardeners and wise seasonal shoppers like to plan their menus around the fruits and vegetables in season. First we decide to "make something with all those apples," then we decide to bake a pie. I've tried to expand all of my favorite dessert recipes to include variations for any number of fruits or vegetables that might be in season. So if you think you'd like to make a honey cake, you'll find a recipe with variations for making it with cherries, or sweet potatoes, or zucchini, or green tomatoes, or blueberries, or blackberries, or raspberries— whichever you happen to have on hand. Many of the desserts can be made with canned or frozen fruits that you have put by, if you don't have fresh fruits in the house.

There is a special emphasis on fruits in this cookbook. Fruits contribute a natural sweetness so most fruit desserts require less sugar.

Less sugar, more garden-grown goodness: that's the theme of this cookbook. I hope you'll enjoy it.

Fruits and Vegetables

When the garden bounty begins to get out of hand, I turn some of my surplus fruits and vegetables into quick purees which can be frozen and later transformed into sauces or desserts. Many of my ideas for handling purees come from Garden Way's *Easy Harvest Sauce and Puree Cookbook* by Marjorie Blanchard, and you may want to consult that book for more ideas.

Most vegetables are precooked before they are pureed; with fruits, it varies. A food processor fitted with a steel blade, a blender, or a food mill, such as the Squeezo strainer, is needed for making the purees.

When a recipe in the book calls for a vegetable puree, check the chart that follows for yield information and cooking advice. If your apple sauce or pear sauce is runny, thicken it by cooking it over a low heat until it reaches the desired consistency. Stir often to prevent scorching. For the recipes in this book, the apple sauce and pear sauce should be thick enough to require spooning from the jar.

Prevent Browning

Many fruits (apples, peaches, pears) brown when exposed to the air. You can prevent this by treating the fruit with ascorbic acid (vitamin C) or citric acid (lemon juice). Usually I slice my fruit into water to which I have added a couple of tablespoons of lemon juice. Sometimes I spray a water/lemon juice mist over the fruit. Precise measurement of the lemon juice is not necessary. You can also use commercially available ascorbic acid for the same results. Purchase the ascorbic acid at a drug store and use according to the manufacturers' recommendations.

More Handling Information

Even the best gardener, in the most ideal climate, won't be growing all of the fruits and vegetables we have included in this cookbook. Fortunately, fresh fruit is available year-round at most supermarkets.

Whether the produce is still on the vine or sitting in a refrigerated display case, you want only the fruits and vegetables that are at their prime eating stage.

GUIDE TO MAKING PUREES

Fruit or Vegetable	Yield	Method
Apples	1 pound = 2 cups puree	Cook quartered, unpeeled apples in a small amount of water until tender; process through food mill.
Beans, White	⅔ pound (2 cups cooked) = 2 cups puree	Cook until very soft. Process in blender or food processor.
Beets	1 pound (3 cups cooked) = 2 cups puree	Cook until tender. Peel. Process in blender or food processor.
Blackberries	2 cups = 1 cup puree	Process in a blender, food processor, or food mill. Strain to remove seeds.
Blueberries	2 cups = 1 cup puree	Pick over and remove stems. Process in a blender or food processor.
Carrots	1 pound = 2 cups puree	Cook in a small amount of water until tender. Process in blender, food mill, or food processor.
Cherries	1 pound (pitted) = 1¾ cups puree	Remove pits and puree in blender or food processor until smooth.
Eggplant	1 pound = ¾ cup puree	Cook until very tender. Drain excess moisture and mash with fork.

GUIDE TO MAKING PUREES

(continued)

Fruit or Vegetable	Yield	Method
Parsnips	1 pound = 2 cups puree	Cook until very tender. Process in a blender, food mill, or food processor.
Peaches	1 pound = 1 cup puree	Peel, pit, and process in a blender or food processor. Add a little lemon juice to the puree to prevent browning.
Pears	1 pound = 1 cup puree	Cook peeled, quartered, and cored pears in small amount of water until tender. Process in a blender or food processor. Add a little lemon juice to the puree to prevent browning.
Plums	1 pound = 1 cup puree	Halve plums, remove pits, and process in a blender or food processor. If desired, plunge whole plums in boiling water for 30 seconds to loosen skin. Then peel, pit, and puree.
Pumpkins	2 pounds = 2 cups puree	Split pumpkin in half, remove seeds, place upside down in 1″ of water in a baking dish. Bake 30–45 minutes until tender. Scoop out the flesh and puree in a blender, food processor, or food mill.
Raspberries	3 cups = 1½ cups puree	Puree in blender, food mill, or food processor. Strain to remove seeds.
Rhubarb	1 pound = 2 cups puree	Cook in a small amount of water until tender. Process in a blender, food mill, or food processor.
Strawberries	3 cups = 2 cups puree	Hull berries, process in a blender or food processor.
Sweet Potatoes	1 pound = 2 cups puree	Cook potatoes in water to cover until tender. Drain, peel, and put through food mill or food processor.
Winter Squash	1 pound = 2 cups puree	Split in half, remove seeds, and cook until tender. Scoop out flesh. Process in a food mill, blender, or food processor.

CHOOSING AND STORING FRUITS AND VEGETABLES

Fruits and Vegetables	What to Look For	How to Store	Preparation Tips
Apples	Firm, well-colored fruits; avoid shriveled skins, soft fruit, brown spots.	Store in a cool, dark, airy place; keep for several months.	Treat sliced fruit with ascorbic or citric acid to prevent browning. Unpeeled apples give baked goods a pinkish tinge.
Beans, White	Also called navy beans or pea beans.	Store dried beans in a cool dark place; keep indefinitely.	
Beets	Smooth, small to medium-size beets with no ridges or blemishes.	Remove tops, leaving 1 inch of stem. Refrigerate tops and roots in the crisper or wrapped in the refrigerator; use within 2–3 weeks.	Cook unpeeled in boiling water for 30–45 minutes.
Blackberries	Plump, uniform color; avoid crushed fruit, stained cartons, berries with green caps and stems attached.	Refrigerate unwashed; keep 1–2 days; taste best within hours of picking.	Wash as quickly as possible, handle gently.
Blueberries	Plump, blue berries with "silvery" cast to the skin; avoid crushed fruit, stained cartons.	Refrigerate, use within 2–3 days; taste best within hours of picking.	Pick off all the stems, wash quickly, handle gently.
Carrots	Firm, bright-colored carrots; avoid limp, shriveled carrots.	Remove tops, refrigerate in crisper or wrapped in refrigerator 1–2 weeks.	Baby carrots are the sweetest tasting and don't need peeling.

CHOOSING AND STORING FRUITS AND VEGETABLES

(continued)

Fruits and Vegetables	What to Look For	How to Store	Preparation Tips
Cherries	Plump fruit; glossy skins; avoid soft, shriveled fruits or stems. Sweet cherries should be dark red in color.	Refrigerate; use within 2–3 days.	Cherry pitters are convenient; paring knives work well, too.
Eggplant	Plump, uniform color; flesh yields slightly to pressure.	Refrigerate; use within 1–2 days.	Salting rids eggplant of excess moisture. Rinse well after salting.
Grapes	Firm fruit, grapes well attached to stems; avoid soft fruit, shriveled or brittle stems.	Refrigerate, use within 1–2 weeks.	To seed Concord grapes, pinch, and the seed will pop out.
Kiwi Fruit	Fuzzy skin, fruit yields somewhat to the touch; avoid fruit with soft spots.	Refrigerate ripe fruit; use within 1–2 days.	Peel with a vegetable peeler.
Lemons	Bright, heavy fruit; avoid soft, shriveled, or hard skins.	Refrigerate, use within 2 weeks.	To get more juice from a lemon (or any citrus fruit) drop it into hot water, then roll between your hands, slice, and squeeze.
Melons	Fruit yields slightly to touch, pleasant "musky" aroma (except casabas).	Melons are best vine ripened. Unripe cantaloupes will ripen at room temperatures; honeydew will not.	To prevent softening, slice just before serving. Store ripe melons in the refrigerator and use within 2–3 days.
Parsnips	Smooth, well-shaped roots.	Refrigerate unwashed in crisper or in perforated plastic bags; keep 4–5 weeks.	

CHOOSING AND STORING FRUITS AND VEGETABLES
(continued)

Fruits and Vegetables	What to Look For	How to Store	Preparation Tips
Peaches	Fruit yields slightly to the touch, yellow or cream color, avoid green, shriveled, or bruised fruit.	Refrigerate and use in 3–5 days.	Treat with ascorbic or citric acid to prevent browning. To peel, blanch in boiling water for 30 seconds, then plunge into cold water. This loosens the skin and makes peeling easy.
Pears	Fairly firm fruit; avoid shriveled, discolored, or bruised fruits.	Store at room temperature to ripen and use in 3–5 days; or individually wrap and store in cool, dark place. If the skin looks intact but the flesh has browned, the fruit has been exposed to too low temperatures.	Use a vegetable peeler to peel; treat sliced fruit with ascorbic or citric acid to prevent browning.
Plums	Plump fruit; avoid hard, shriveled, cracked, or bruised fruit.	Refrigerate, use within 3–5 days.	
Pumpkins	Bright orange color, stems attached.	Store in cool, dark place; use within 1–2 months.	A raw pumpkin yields half its weight in usable flesh.
Sweet Potatoes	Plump, firm potatoes with no bruises or soft spots.	Store in cool, dark place; use within 1 week.	Most "yams" in the supermarket are really sweet potatoes.

CHOOSING AND STORING FRUITS AND VEGETABLES

(continued)

Fruits and Vegetables	What to Look For	How to Store	Preparation Tips
Raspberries	Plump fruit, avoid crushed fruit, stained cartons, berries with green hull and stem attached.	Refrigerate, use within 1–2 days; taste best within hours of picking.	Wash briefly, handle gently.
Rhubarb	Firm, crisp, red or green stalks, smaller stalks tend to be sweeter; avoid soft flabby stalks.	Refrigerate in crisper, or wrapped in perforated plastic bags; use within 3–5 days.	String only if old and woody.
Strawberries	Plump, red berries; avoid shriveled or soft berries, stained containers.	Refrigerate, use within 1–2 days. Taste best within hours of picking.	Wash briefly, hull with a strawberry huller or a paring knife.
Summer Squash	Young, 4–8″ squash with unblemished skin.	Refrigerate in crisper or perforated plastic bags; use within 3–4 days.	Grate, and allow to drain in a colander for 30 minutes to eliminate excess moisture.
Watermelon	The spot where the watermelon rested on the ground turns from white to deep creamy yellow when ripe. Or the watermelon will make a sharp, not muffled, sound when you thump it.	Store at room temperature 2–3 days and refrigerate before serving.	Slice just before serving, serve well chilled.
Winter Squash	Hard, heavy, unblemished squash.	Store in a cool, dark place; will keep 1–2 months.	Butternut and hubbard are especially good in desserts.

Featuring Fruits

The central focus of each dessert in this chapter is fruit. The fruit isn't wrapped in dough, or pureed into the background of a batter. It stands on its own: fruit in combination with other fruits, fruits lightly dressed with a liqueur or whipped cream, or fruit served just plain. Some are lightly cooked, some are served with a cooked sauce. But in each case, the strong, fresh flavor of the fruit is the dominant taste.

This is an idea chapter as well as a recipe chapter. I want to share with you some of my ideas for presenting fruits in glamorous, elegant ways. Recreate my serving ideas, or use them for stepping stones toward your own creative fruit desserts.

Fresh Fruit Combinations

Desserts don't have to be baked to be wonderful. Here are some serving suggestions for presenting fresh fruits in their natural glory.

Make peach melbas with layers of sliced peaches, vanilla ice cream, and sweetened raspberry puree.

Layer berries, melon balls, and sliced peaches, pears, or apples in champagne glasses and top with a fruit sauce (pages 142–145) or with whipped cream.

Layer sliced fruits or berries with ice cream or whipped cream in parfait glasses.

Arrange whole strawberries, melon cubes, and peach or pear slices on bamboo skewers. Dress with a Lime and Honey Sauce (page 15) or serve with a Chocolate Fondue Sauce (page 146).

Fill an attractive shallow serving dish with sifted confectioners' sugar. Arrange whole strawberries in the sugar with the stems facing up.

Place whole strawberries in a straw basket lined with leaves. Serve with a side dish of sifted confectioners' sugar.

Cut a honeydew and a cantaloupe into wedges and remove the seeds. With a melon baller, scoop out 3 melon balls from each wedge. Place the honeydew balls in the cantaloupe wedges and the cantaloupe balls in the honeydew wedges. Decorate with sprigs of mint and wedges of lime.

Serve fresh fruit with cheese: wedges of watermelon with feta cheese, slices of apples with cheddar cheese, slices of pears with blue cheese, slices of peaches with cream cheese sweetened with raspberry jam.

Make a Pear Porcupine by poaching pears in light syrup (see Compotes, page 28) until tender, about 10 minutes. Stick almond slivers into the pear. Pour Chocolate Fondue Sauce (page 146) over the pears and serve.

Sauté apples, pears, or peaches in a little butter and mix in red currant jelly, orange marmalade, ginger marmalade, raspberry jam or jelly, or apricot jam.

Heat your favorite home preserve with a little water, orange juice, or liquor and pour over sliced fruits.

Fruit Salads

At the height of the fruit season, nothing is more refreshing than a fresh fruit salad, served with a meal or as a dessert. As you prepare the fruits, it is a good idea to slice those fruits which brown quickly into a bowl of water to which you have added a little lemon juice. For best results, mix up the fruit salad just before serving. (After an hour or so, the fruits will become limp and soggy and the lemon juice will lose its ability to prevent browning.)

When you are ready to serve, toss the fruits with one of the following light sauces.

Sauces

Lime and Honey Sauce. Squeeze the juice from 2 limes and sweeten to taste with honey. Grate the rind of 1 lime and add to the sauce.

Orange Sauce. Mix orange juice with vanilla or almond extract or rosewater.

Orange and Maple Sauce. Sweeten some orange juice with a small amount of maple syrup to taste. Grate the rind of half an orange into the sauce.

Mint and Lemon Sauce. Squeeze the juice from 1 or 2 lemons, sweeten to taste with honey. Add ¼ cup water or orange juice and ¼ cup fresh mint leaves. Combine all the ingredients in a blender and blend until the mint is chopped.

Spirit Sauce. For every 2 cups of fruit salad, pour 1 tablespoon (or to taste) of any of the following: rum, Southern Comfort, port, sweet red or white wine, crème de cassis, champagne, Grand Marnier, sweet cream sherry, Madeira, kirsch, sauterne, Cointreau, or Medori. For more flavor, marinate the fruit in the spirits 2 hours before serving.

Fruit Salad Toppings

Just before serving, top your fruit salad with one of these garnishes or toppings.

Nuts:

Walnuts	Pecans	Hazelnuts
Cashews	Crushed Brazil nuts	Almonds

Flowers:

Violas

Rose petals

Calendula flowers

Nasturtiums

Pansies

Opal basil blossoms

Herbs:

Lemon verbena leaves, whole or chopped

Mint leaves, whole or chopped

Flavored Sugar:

Rose Geranium Sugar (page 68)

Confectioners' sugar with powdered ginger

Confectioners' sugar with cinnamon

Cinnamon and granulated sugar

Other Sprinkled Toppings:

Shredded coconut

Shredded coconut browned for 3–4 minutes over medium heat

Chocolate chips

Chocolate sprinkles

Chocolate shavings

Currants

Raisins

Chopped dates

Chopped crystallized ginger

Grated lemon or orange peels

Slivered lemon or orange peels

Sauce Toppings:

Fruit sherbet

Ice cream

Vanilla ice cream flavored with marmalade

Sweetened whipped cream flavored with liqueur, cocoa, or spices

Sour cream, plain or sweetened with jam or maple syrup

Yogurt, plain or sweetened with jam or maple syrup or brown sugar

Cream cheese thinned with apricot or raspberry jam or marmalade.

Spirited Fruits

A little liquor sprinkled on fresh fruits draws the juices from the fruit and makes a lovely sauce. You can sprinkle one of the Spirit Sauces (page 15) on plain sliced fruits, or try one of these desserts.

Cold Desserts

Fill a cantaloupe half with port wine.

Remove a small piece from a whole watermelon. Pour in rum or vodka and replace the piece of melon. Refrigerate for at least 4 hours before serving. Slice the watermelon as usual and serve.

Hot Desserts

Sauté peeled and sliced apples, peaches, or pears in butter with honey or brown sugar and sherry, Madeira, sweet wine, or any other liquor until the fruit is soft.

Sauté peeled and sliced apples, peaches, or pears in butter and flambé with rum, Southern Comfort, or Grand Marnier.

Pour hot apple sauce flavored with liquor and enriched with a little melted butter over gingerbread.

Edible Fruit Baskets

Fruit salad, whole berries, sliced fruits, and melon balls become very special desserts when served in a natural fruit basket. Here are a few ideas.

Serve fruit salad in apple cups. To make the apple cups, remove about ½–¾" off the top of each apple. Carve out the cores and a

apple basket

melon ring

good part of the flesh of each apple. Add the apple flesh to the fruit salad. Treat the insides of the apples with lemon juice to prevent browning and fill with fruit.

Fill melon rings with whole berries, sliced fruits, ice cream, or sherbet. To make the melon rings, remove 1″ from the top and bottom of a whole melon. Set the melon on one of the flat ends and cut away the skin, following the contours of the melon. Turn the melon on its side and cut it into 4–6 rings. Remove the seeds from each ring and place each ring on an individual serving dish and fill.

Fill melon halves with fruits and fruit salads.

Serve fruit salad, strawberries, blueberries, raspberries, or grapes in melon crowns. To make a melon crown, turn the melon on its side and remove about 2″ from the stem end so the melon will stand and the center of the melon is exposed. Remove the seeds. Place the melon on your cutting board cut side up. Peel away the skin following the contours of the melon. Set the melon on its flat side. From the top of the melon, remove triangles of melon that are 1½–2″ wide at the top and come to a point 3–4″ down toward the middle of the melon. Fill the center of the melon with fruit.

Hide a mound of fruit salad or berries beneath a cap of cantaloupe and honeydew wedges and serve on a brunch buffet. To make the melon cap, select a cantaloupe and a honeydew; the melons should be similar in size. Peel the skins, following the contours of the melons. Slice each melon in half lengthwise and scoop out the seeds. Cut the melons into wedges about 1½ inches thick. Slice each wedge in half. On a large round serving plate, place a piece of honeydew with the flat cut on the plate and the curving tip in the air. Place a piece of cantaloupe beside it. Alternate slices of honeydew and cantaloupe to make a round cap. Before the last piece of melon is put

melon cap

into place, fill the cavity with fruit salad or blueberries. Put the last slice of melon in place and top with a strawberry.

Fill chocolate cups with fresh berries and top with a dollop of whipped cream. To make 6 chocolate cups, melt 6 squares of semi-sweet chocolate in the top of a double boiler over, but not in, boiling water. Before you start, be sure the pot is completely dry and that no water gets into the chocolate. Line a muffin tin with paper liners. Take a knife and spread the melted chocolate all over the inside of the muffin papers so that the chocolate is about ¼″ thick. Chill the chocolate until set. Working quickly, but carefully, peel off the paper liners, leaving a chocolate cup. Refrigerate the cups again until you are ready to serve. Fill with berries and decorate with whipped cream. Each cup holds about ¼ cup prepared fruit.

Watermelon Art

Watermelons make wonderful baskets for fruits and can be used as very showy centerpieces on buffet tables. Carved watermelons are surprisingly easy to make. Here are instructions for a Watermelon

Basket, a Watermelon Heart, and a Watermelon Bird. The instructions will be easier to follow if you study the drawings of the finished melons first.

Watermelon Basket

Select a large, unblemished watermelon for the basket. Set the melon on its side. Mark out a handle that is 3″ wide and bisects the melon in the middle. Mark out a second line lengthwise all the way around the middle of the melon. This line is perpendicular to the handle. With a long-bladed knife, make a series of V-shaped cuts evenly around the melon, following the second line, but leaving the handle intact. You have now outlined a basket and handle. Cut away the unwanted melon in sections. Scoop out the pulp and use it for your fruit salad. Fill the basket with fruit salad or melon balls and serve.

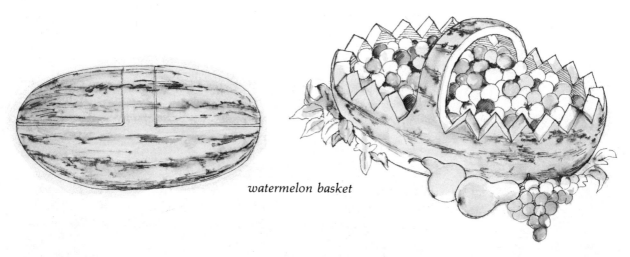

watermelon basket

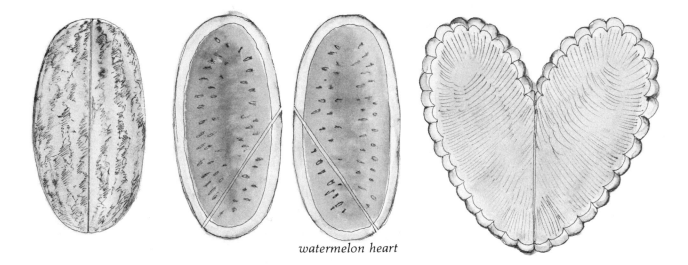

watermelon heart

Watermelon Heart

For this showy centerpiece, you will shape 2 halves of a large, long, evenly shaped melon into a heart. Cut the melon in half lengthwise. Remove a third of one of the melon halves along a diagonal line as shown. Remove the opposite third from the other melon half. Scoop out the fruit, leaving the shell. With a small paring knife, make half-circle cuts around the edges of the shells to make a scalloped edge. Using bamboo skewers (which are available at most specialty food stores), skewer the 2 melon halves together, joining at the diagonal cuts. Fill the melon heart with fruit salad and serve.

Watermelon Bird

Choose a large oval watermelon. Cut a small piece of melon from the stem so that the melon can stand on end. Place the watermelon on its side. With a sharp knife, mark out the silhouette of a peacock in the top half of the melon, as shown. Carefully carve around this

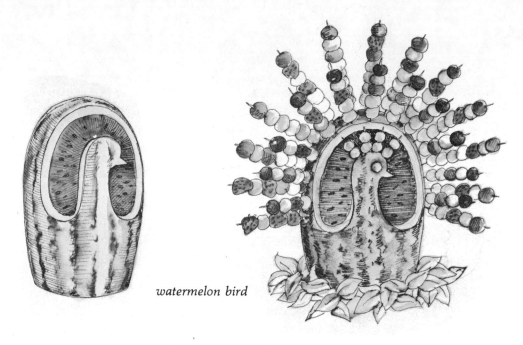

watermelon bird

outline. Remove the unwanted melon from the front around the outline, but leave the back half of the pulp and rind intact. Scoop out the watermelon pulp and make melon balls. Arrange different colored melon balls and strawberries on bamboo skewers. Use the same pattern of colors for each skewer. Stick the skewers around the watermelon to create a fan of colors like the feathers of a peacock.

Recipes

The recipes that follow are all light desserts that feature fruit. Many of these simple fruit dishes can be enriched with the sauces presented in Sauces, Mincemeats. and Butters

Pear and Grape Surprise

PREPARATION TIME: 15 MINUTES
YIELD: 2 SERVINGS

4 ounces cream cheese
4 teaspoons brown sugar
  (optional)
1 peeled ripe pear, cut in half
  and cored
2 grape leaves
2 cups grapes, cut in half
  lengthwise

Mix the cream cheese and the brown sugar together.

Place each pear half on a grape leaf on an individual serving plate, cut side down. Divide the cream cheese mixture evenly between the pear halves and press the mixture onto the outside of each pear half, covering it completely. Press the grapes into the cream cheese in even rows starting at one end of the pear and covering the entire surface. The pear will then look like a bunch of grapes.

Ginger Grapes

PREPARATION TIME: 15 MINUTES
YIELD: 6 SERVINGS

2 pounds grapes
2 egg whites
½ cup confectioners' sugar
1 teaspoon ginger

A very simple and elegant dessert. You may want to add to each serving plate honeydew slices with lime juice squeezed over them.

Cut the grapes into small portion-size bunches.

Beat the egg whites slightly and dip each bunch of grapes into the whites, brushing off the excess on the edge of the bowl. Place the grapes on a cooling rack or cookie sheet.

Mix together the confectioners' sugar and ginger. Sift the sugar over the grapes and refrigerate for at least ½ hour. Serve the grapes on grape leaves, if desired.

Blueberries and Cantaloupe With Cassis Sauce

PREPARATION TIME: 15 MINUTES
YIELD: 4 SERVINGS

1 large ripe cantaloupe
2 cups blueberries
¼ cup crème de cassis

Cut the melon in half lengthwise and scoop out the seeds. Using a melon baller, scoop out melon balls.

Place 1 cup of blueberries in a blender with the cassis. Blend until smooth. Mix the remaining blueberries in with the cantaloupe balls. Pour the sauce over the fruit. Serve immediately.

Rosy Poached Pears

PREPARATION TIME: 15 MINUTES
COOKING TIME: 10–15 MINUTES
YIELD: 6 SERVINGS

6 firm ripe pears
juice of 1 lemon
2 cups dry red wine
1 cup sugar or ½ cup honey
10 whole cloves
3 cinnamon sticks
35 black peppercorns

As you peel the pears, leaving the stems intact, place the pears in a bowl of water to cover with the lemon juice to prevent them from turning brown. If you like, core the pears from the bottom, removing as little of the fruit as possible.

Combine the remaining ingredients in a saucepan that is big enough to hold the pears without letting them touch each other. Bring the ingredients to a boil and stir until the sugar is dissolved. Place the pears in the pan and cover it. Let the pears poach for 10–15 minutes or just until tender. With a slotted spoon, carefully remove the pears from the syrup. Strain the syrup and return it to the pan. Boil the syrup until it thickens. Spoon the syrup over the pears and serve warm or cold.

Baked Stuffed Apples

PREPARATION TIME: 15 MINUTES
BAKING TIME: 30 MINUTES
YIELD: 1 APPLE PER PERSON

Preheat the oven to 350° F.

Remove the cores from as many apples as people you are serving. Place the apples in a baking dish and pour in enough water, cider, or wine to cover the bottom of the dish with ¼" liquid.

Combine the ingredients for the filling (choose from the list below) and fill the apples. Dot with butter, if desired. Bake the apples for 30 minutes. Baste the apples with the baking liquid several times during the baking.

Serve hot or cold, alone or with Custard Sauce (page 141), Lemon Curd Sauce (page 144), Cider Sauce (page 145), ice cream, or whipped cream.

Fillings:
- Chopped prunes or dates, nuts, and raspberry jam.
- Green Tomato Mincemeat (page 147) or Pear Mincemeat (page 148).
- Apple Butter (page 149), bread crumbs, and raisins.
- Macaroon crumbs, cider, and cinnamon.
- Brown sugar, butter, cinnamon, and raisins.
- Coconut, honey, and dates.
- Almonds and currant jelly.
- Raisins and marmalade.
- Dates and orange juice.
- Cookie crumbs, jam, and currants.

Baked Peaches

PREPARATION TIME: 10 MINUTES
BAKING TIME: 10–15 MINUTES
YIELD: 1 PEACH PER PERSON

Preheat the oven to 350° F.

Peel the peaches by dropping them into boiling water for 30 seconds and then plunging them into cold water. The skins should be loosened and slip off easily. Split the peaches in half and remove the pit. Place the peaches in a baking dish, cut side up. Drizzle melted butter and maple syrup, honey, or brown sugar over the peaches. Pour ½″ orange juice or water into the bottom of the baking dish. Bake the peaches for 10–15 minutes.

To vary this dessert, stuff the peaches with any of the fillings listed under Baked Stuffed Apples (page 25) or serve with one of the sauces presented on pages 141–45.

Stewed Rhubarb

PREPARATION TIME: 10 MINUTES
COOKING TIME: 15 MINUTES
YIELD: 3 CUPS

4 cups fresh or frozen
  rhubarb, cut in 1″ pieces
½ cup water
½ cup honey or sugar

Serve Stewed Rhubarb plain, with ice cream, or over biscuits or gingerbread.

Combine all the ingredients in a medium-size saucepan and simmer until the rhubarb is tender. Add more water if necessary.

Pears Poached in Grand Marnier

PREPARATION TIME: 15 MINUTES
COOKING TIME: 15 MINUTES
YIELD: 6 SERVINGS

6 firm, unblemished pears
2 tablespoons lemon juice
2 cups water
1 cup sugar
½ cup red currant jelly
1 tablespoon lemon juice
2 cinnamon sticks
5 whole cloves
¼ cup Grand Marnier

Peel the pears, leaving the stems in place. Place the pears in a bowl of water to cover with the lemon juice to prevent them from browning. Fit the pears into a saucepan that is large enough to hold the pears without having them touch each other. Combine the water, sugar, jelly, and 1 tablespoon lemon juice and pour this mixture over the pears. Add the cinnamon sticks and cloves to the cooking liquid. Simmer the pears gently for 10–15 minutes, until they are just tender. Remove the pears carefully with a slotted spoon. Bring the syrup to a boil and simmer it for a few minutes. Strain the syrup and return it to the pan. Stir in the Grand Marnier and pour the syrup over the pears. Serve warm or cold.

Compotes

PREPARATION TIME: 10 MINUTES
COOKING TIME: 10–15 MINUTES
YIELD: 6 SERVINGS

Compotes are fruits cooked briefly—just until tender—in a sweetened syrup and then chilled. Compotes can be made with combinations of peeled and sliced apples, seeded grapes, peeled and sliced peaches, sliced apricots, peeled and sliced pears, pitted cherries, sliced rhubarb, and quartered plums. Here are some recipes.

Compote With Light Syrup. Combine 4 cups prepared fruit with 1 cup sugar, honey, or maple syrup, 3 cups water, 1 unpeeled lemon slice, and 1 cinnamon stick. Simmer until the fruit is tender. Chill.

Compote With Medium Syrup. Combine 4 cups prepared fruit with 1 cup sugar, honey, or maple syrup, 2 cups water, and 1 unpeeled lemon slice. In a muslin spice bag, combine 1 cinnamon stick, 6 whole cloves, and 4 allspice berries. Add to the syrup and simmer until the fruit is tender. Remove the spice bag. Chill.

Compote With Heavy Syrup. Combine 4 cups prepared fruit with 1½ cups white or brown sugar, honey, or maple syrup; 1½ cups water; and 1 unpeeled lemon slice. In a muslin spice bag, combine 1 cinnamon stick, 6 whole cloves, and 4 allspice berries. Add to the syrup and simmer until the fruit is tender. Remove the spice bag. Chill.

Soufflés, Mousses, Custards, and Puddings

If you are concerned about the amount of sugar or honey you bake with, please read on. Most of these recipes call for less sweeteners than other desserts do. The Pear Almond Mousse, the Apple Mousse, and the Jeweled White Grape Juice Mold rely on the natural sweetness of fruit, with no added sugar. Other desserts call for just a little honey or sugar. Of course, there are a few desserts that call for a lot of sugar, as well as eggs and cream—those special occasion desserts we all delight in.

The word "soufflé" is the past tense of the French verb *souffler*, which means to puff up. The cold soufflés in this book are more like mousses, made with eggs and gelatin; they don't puff up because they are not baked. Sometimes these desserts are presented as traditional French soufflés towering high above the serving dish. This is done with a collar.

Making a Soufflé Collar

To make a collar, cut a length of aluminum foil long enough to go around the outside of your straight-sided soufflé dish, leaving a 3″ overlap. Fold the foil in half lengthwise. Wrap the collar around the soufflé dish so that the collar rises 3″ above the sides of the dish. Secure with tape. Pour the soufflé into the dish and chill until firm. Just before serving, remove the collar. The result is a very dramatic, towering dessert.

Unmolding Gelatin Desserts

To unmold a gelatin dessert, prepare your serving plate by wetting it with water. This allows you to slide the dessert to center it on the plate, if necessary. Next, run warm water (not hot) into a large bowl or in your sink. Dip the mold into the warm water to the depth of the gelatin for about 15 seconds, being careful not to spill water onto the dessert. Loosen the gelatin around the edge of the mold with the tip of a paring knife. Place the serving dish on top of the mold and hold it firmly. Carefully turn the mold and plate over together. Gently shake the mold until the gelatin comes loose. If the gelatin does not come loose right away, repeat the warm water bath briefly. Center the mold on the plate and lift off the mold. Garnish with fruit slices, a sauce, or whipped cream, and serve.

Ginger Cantaloupe Dessert

PREPARATION TIME: 20 MINUTES
CHILLING TIME: 3 HOURS
YIELD: 5 SERVINGS

2 tablespoons gelatin
¼ cup water
1 large cantaloupe
1 cup orange juice
1 tablespoon sugar, honey,
   or maple syrup
1 tablespoon crystallized
   ginger
¼ cup lime juice

Sprinkle the gelatin over the water and set aside for 5 minutes.

Peel and seed the cantaloupe and cut it into cubes. Puree the cantaloupe in a food processor or blender with the orange juice, sweetener, ginger, and lime juice until smooth.

Then heat the gelatin gently until melted. Stir the gelatin into the melon mixture and pour into a 4-cup or 5-cup mold. Chill until set. Serve with blueberries or the Blueberry Orange Sauce (page 143).

Chinese Almond Float With Berries

PREPARATION TIME: 15 MINUTES
CHILLING TIME: 3 HOURS
YIELD: 6–8 SERVINGS

1 tablespoon gelatin
3 cups water
¼ cup sugar or honey
 (optional)
⅔ cup condensed milk
1½ teaspoons almond extract
2½ cups water
3 cups strawberries, blueberries, blackberries, or
 raspberries
2 tablespoons rum
 (optional)

In a small saucepan, sprinkle the gelatin over ½ cup water. Set aside.

In a medium-size mixing bowl, combine the sweetener, milk, almond extract, and the remaining 2½ cups water.

Gently heat the gelatin until it melts. Mix the gelatin into the milk mixture.

Rinse a 9″ × 13″ baking dish with tap water and do not dry it. Pour in the milk mixture. Place the pan in the refrigerator and chill until firm.

While the float sets, slice the strawberries and marinate in 2 tablespoons rum if desired.

When the float has set, cut the gelatin into 1″ diamonds by cutting on the diagonal in one direction and lengthwise in another direction. Carefully spoon the diamonds into serving dishes and spoon on the fruit.

Variations

Chinese Almond Float With Peaches. Substitute 3 cups of peeled and sliced peaches for the berries.

Chinese Almond Float With Pears. Substitute 3 cups of peeled and sliced pears for the berries.

Chinese Almond Float With Plums. Substitute 3 cups of quartered plums for the berries.

Peach Yogurt Mousse

PREPARATION TIME: 30 MINUTES
CHILLING TIME: 3 HOURS
YIELD: 4–6 SERVINGS

1 tablespoon gelatin
¼ cup cold water
4 egg whites
⅓ cup honey
2½ cups peach puree
  (page 5)
2 tablespoons fresh lemon
  juice
1½ cups plain yogurt

Sprinkle the gelatin over the water in a small saucepan and set aside.

Whip the egg whites until frothy. Slowly add the honey and continue beating the egg whites until they are stiff.

Mix together the peaches, lemon juice, and yogurt.

Over very low heat, heat the gelatin until just melted. Fold the peaches and gelatin into the egg whites. Pour the mousse into a 1½-quart mold and refrigerate until set. Unmold and serve.

Variations

Strawberry Yogurt Mousse. Substitute 2½ cups strawberry puree (page 5) for the peaches.

Blackberry Yogurt Mousse. Strain 2½ cups blackberry puree (page 4) to remove the seeds. Substitute the strained puree for the peaches.

Raspberry Yogurt Mousse. Strain 2½ cups raspberry puree (page 5) to remove the seeds. Substitute the strained raspberry puree for the peaches.

Fresh Strawberry Ricotta Mousse

PREPARATION TIME: 20 MINUTES
CHILLING TIME: 3 HOURS
YIELD: 6 SERVINGS

1 tablespoon gelatin
⅓ cup water
1 pound ricotta cheese
¼ cup honey
1 tablespoon lemon juice
1 teaspoon grated lemon rind
1 tablespoon Grand Marnier
   or rum (optional)
3 cups hulled strawberries

In a small saucepan, sprinkle the gelatin over the water and set it aside.

Place the ricotta cheese in a food processor or mixing bowl, add the honey, and whip together.

Add the lemon juice, lemon rind, and liqueur to the ricotta mixture.

Gently heat the gelatin mixture over low heat until the gelatin is melted.

Blend the gelatin into the ricotta mixture thoroughly.

If you are using a food processor, add the strawberries to the ricotta mixture in the processor, and process for a few seconds to incorporate the strawberries but not to completely break them up. If you are using a mixer, crush the strawberries, then add them to the ricotta and blend them in.

You can use frozen unsweetened strawberries in this mousse. In your food processor or blender, process the strawberries first while still slightly frozen. Then set aside and mix the ricotta and honey. When mixing the frozen strawberries into the ricotta, add a little of the strawberries into the ricotta-gelatin mixture and stir it gently to prevent the gelatin from congealing instantly.

Pour the mixture into a 5-cup mold and chill until set. Serve with additional strawberries if desired, or with strawberry puree sweetened with honey.

Blackberry Bavarian Cream

PREPARATION TIME: 45 MINUTES
CHILLING TIME: 3 HOURS
YIELD: 8 SERVINGS

Fruited Bavarian creams are deliciously creamy molded desserts made with a combination of eggs, cream, gelatin, and fruit. They are chilled until firm in a mold, or sometimes combined with lady fingers or jelly rolls in a springform pan or a deep bowl to make fruit charlottes, or spread between the layers of a genoise cake.

The classical way to serve Bavarian creams is in a soufflé dish that has a collar tied around it, extending the top of the dish. The collar is removed when the cream has set. Bavarian creams are delicious frozen.

3 cups blackberries
¾ cup sugar
1 tablespoon gelatin
3 tablespoons cold water
3 tablespoons boiling water
2 egg whites
1 cup whipping cream

In a medium-size mixing bowl, combine the blackberries and sugar. Crush the berries with the back of a spoon. Let the berries sit for 30 minutes. Strain to remove the seeds if desired.

Sprinkle the gelatin on the cold water and allow it to sit for about 5 minutes. Then pour in the boiling water and stir until the gelatin is dissolved.

Whip the egg whites until stiff. Then whip the cream until stiff. Combine all the ingredients, and fold together gently. Pour the Bavarian cream into a 1½-quart mold and chill for several hours before unmolding. Serve immediately.

Variations

Raspberry Bavarian Cream. Substitute 3 cups of raspberries for the blackberries.

Strawberry Bavarian Cream. Substitute 3 cups of sliced strawberries for the blackberries.

Peach Bavarian Cream. Substitute 3 cups of peeled, sliced peaches for the blackberries. Chop the peaches or process briefly in a food processor.

Cherry Bavarian Cream. Substitute 3 cups of pitted sweet cherries for the blackberries. Chop the cherries or process briefly in a food processor.

Pear Almond Mousse

PREPARATION TIME: 15 MINUTES
CHILLING TIME: 3 HOURS
YIELD: 5–6 SERVINGS

In only 15 minutes, you can whip up this sugar-free, elegant dessert. The fruit and grape juice contribute a natural sweetness.

2 tablespoons gelatin
¼ cup cold water
5–6 pears, peeled, cored, and chopped (about 3 cups)
1 cup white grape juice
¼ teaspoon almond extract

Sprinkle the gelatin over the water in a small saucepan and set aside.

Combine the pears, grape juice, and almond extract in a food processor or blender. Blend until smooth.

Heat the gelatin gently until it is melted. Add the gelatin mixture to the pears. Mix well. Pour into a 3-cup mold and chill until firm. Serve from the mold with strawberries or blueberries if desired.

Danish Red Berry Pudding

PREPARATION TIME: 20 MINUTES
CHILLING TIME: 3 HOURS
YIELD: 6 SERVINGS

1 cup raspberries
2 cups strawberries
1 cup plus 3 tablespoons cold water
3 tablespoons cornstarch
¼ cup honey or sugar or to taste

Combine the strawberries and raspberries in a food processor or a blender and blend until pureed. Strain the berry mixture to remove the seeds. Combine the berries with 1 cup water in a medium-size saucepan.

Blend the cornstarch with 3 tablespoons water in a small bowl or cup, making sure there are no lumps. Pour the cornstarch mixture into the berries with the sweetener. Cook on medium heat until the mixture thickens, about 8 minutes. Pour the berry pudding into a serving dish or individual dessert cups and cover with plastic film wrap to prevent a skin from forming. Chill until very cold. Serve with whipped cream.

Summer Berry Pudding

PREPARATION TIME: 20 MINUTES
CHILLING TIME: 12 HOURS
YIELD: 8 SERVINGS

1½ **quarts raspberries or blackberries**

¾ **cup honey or to taste**

2 **tablespoons lemon juice**

6 **tablespoons crème de cassis (optional)**

10 **slices white bread with crusts removed**

1 **cup whipping cream**

An easy English dessert that truly captures the exquisite taste of raspberries and blackberries in season. This can also be made with frozen berries.

Place the berries in a blender or food processor and blend until smooth. Pour the puree through a sieve to remove the seeds.

Combine the puree with the honey, lemon juice, and crème de cassis. Adjust the sweetener if necessary.

Line a 2-quart soufflé dish or deep bowl with plastic film wrap. Pour a little of the berry mixture into the dish. Cover with a layer of bread. Pour more berry puree on top and continue layering until the dish is full. End with a piece of bread on top. Set the dish in a larger bowl to catch the drips and weight the pudding with a flat plate with a 2–3-pound weight on top (a filled juice can works well). Refrigerate for at least 12 hours.

When it is time to serve, whip the cream. Invert the pudding onto a serving plate. Decorate the top with rosettes of whipped cream and serve.

Raspberry Cloud Soufflé

PREPARATION TIME: 40 MINUTES
BAKING TIME: 35 MINUTES
YIELD: 6–8 SERVINGS

2 cups bread crumbs
½ cup butter, melted
1 teaspoon cinnamon
¾ cup sugar
2 cups peeled and sliced
  peaches
1 cup raspberry jam
¼ cup butter
⅓ cup unbleached all-
  purpose flour
2 cups milk
1 teaspoon lemon extract
grated rind from 1 lemon
6 egg whites, beaten

Preheat the oven to 400° F. Grease a 2-quart soufflé dish or baking dish.

Mix together the bread crumbs, the ½ cup melted butter, cinnamon, and ¼ cup of the sugar. Place half of this mixture in the bottom of the soufflé dish. Arrange half of the peaches on top of the bread crumbs. Put the jam in the blender and blend until it has a spreading consistency. Pour half of the raspberry jam over the peaches. Sprinkle the remaining bread crumb mixture over the jam, then the remaining peaches and raspberry jam. Set the dish aside.

In a medium-size saucepan, melt ¼ cup butter and stir in the flour, using the back of the spoon to remove any lumps. Slowly add the milk a little at a time and, stirring well after each addition to remove any lumps, add the remaining ½ cup sugar, the lemon extract, and lemon rind. Cook this mixture until it has thickened. Pour into a large mixing bowl and cool the sauce slightly.

Beat the egg whites until stiff. Fold a third of the egg whites into the lemon sauce. Blend thoroughly. Then fold in the remaining egg whites. Pour this mixture on top of the fruit and bake for 35 minutes. Serve warm or cold.

Chocolate Orange Pumpkin Soufflé

PREPARATION TIME: 30 MINUTES
CHILLING TIME: 2 HOURS
YIELD: 8–10 SERVINGS

2 tablespoons gelatin
1½ cups orange juice
¾ cup brown sugar
¼ cup maple syrup
4 egg yolks
2 cups pumpkin puree
(page 5)
1 tablespoon crème de cacao
(optional)
2 ounces semisweet chocolate,
melted
1 teaspoon cinnamon
¼ teaspoon ginger
¼ teaspoon nutmeg
½ teaspoon salt
6 egg whites
¼ cup honey

In a small saucepan, sprinkle the gelatin over the orange juice and set aside.

Mix together the brown sugar, maple syrup, egg yolks, pumpkin puree, crème de cacao, melted chocolate, cinnamon, ginger, nutmeg, and salt.

Melt the gelatin over low heat and add to the pumpkin.

Beat the egg whites until soft peaks appear. Slowly drizzle in the honey and continue beating until stiff peaks appear. Fold a third of the egg white mixture into the pumpkin mixture. Fold in the remaining egg whites. Pour into a 2-quart soufflé dish and chill until firm.

If you would like to make a soufflé that sticks up above the serving dish, you can line the outside of a 1½-quart soufflé dish with the aluminum foil collar described on page 31. Pour in the soufflé and chill.

For a decorative touch, pour the soufflé into individual dessert glasses and top with chocolate filigrees (page 152), then chill.

Variations

Orange Pumpkin Soufflé. Omit the melted chocolate and replace the crème de cacao with 1 tablespoon Grand Marnier.

Chocolate Orange Squash Soufflé. Substitute 2 cups winter squash puree (page 5) for the pumpkin.

Brandied Pumpkin Flan

PREPARATION TIME: 20 MINUTES
BAKING TIME: 1 HOUR
YIELD: 6 SERVINGS

½ cup sugar
1 cup heavy cream
1 cup milk
2 whole eggs
3 egg yolks
⅓ cup sugar or honey
1 teaspoon vanilla extract
1 cup pumpkin puree
  (page 5)
2 tablespoons brandy

Preheat the oven to 350° F.

In a small, heavy-bottomed saucepan, heat the sugar over medium heat until it makes a golden syrup. Carefully pour this caramelized syrup into the bottom of a 4-cup mold and tip the mold to coat the inside with the syrup. Set the mold aside.

Scald the cream and milk. In a mixing bowl, beat together the eggs, egg yolks, sweetener, vanilla, pumpkin, and brandy. Pour in a little hot milk and stir well to temper the eggs. Then mix in the remaining milk. Pour the custard into the mold over the caramelized syrup.

Place the mold in a larger pan of hot water and bake for 1 hour. After the custard is removed from the oven, chill it thoroughly.

Just before serving, dip the mold into hot water for a minute and then invert onto a serving plate with a rim. The caramel will flow down over the custard as a lovely sauce.

Steamed Plum Pudding

PREPARATION TIME: 20 MINUTES
BAKING TIME: 1½ HOURS
YIELD: 6 SERVINGS

1 pound plums
½ cup honey
1 egg
2 tablespoons butter, melted
1 cup unbleached all-purpose flour or ½ cup unbleached all-purpose flour and ½ cup whole wheat flour
1 teaspoon baking soda
½ teaspoon ginger
½ cup currants
½ cup chopped walnuts

In a food processor or blender, puree the plums. Measure out 1 cup plum puree. In a medium-size mixing bowl, combine the puree with the honey, egg, and butter.

Sift together the flour, baking soda, and ginger. Mix the dry ingredients in with the plum mixture. Stir in the currants and nuts. Grease a 1½-quart metal mold or soufflé dish and pour in the batter. Cover the mold with a double layer of aluminum foil tied with a string around the rim to keep it in place.

Place the mold on a rack in a large cooking pot. Pour boiling water around the pudding mold until the water comes two-thirds of the way up the side of the mold. Cover the pot, place over medium heat, and steam the pudding for 1½ hours. Remove the mold from the pot. Allow the pudding to sit for 15 minutes before unmolding.

To unmold, place a serving dish upside down on the mold and invert, gently shaking the pudding. It should slide out.

Serve with Plum Sauce (page 142), Gingered Pear Sauce (page 144), Cider Sauce (page 145), ice cream, or whipped cream.

Variations

Steamed Peach Pudding. Use 1 pound peaches instead of the plums. Peel the peaches before pureeing.

Steamed Blueberry Pudding. Use 2 cups blueberries instead of the plums.

Steamed Pear Pudding. Use 1 pound pears instead of the plums. Peel and core the pears before pureeing.

Steamed Apple Pudding. Use ½ pound apples (2 medium-size apples) instead of the plums. Peel, core, and cook the apples in a small amount of water to soften before pureeing in the food processor.

Cherry Clafouti

PREPARATION TIME: 20 MINUTES
BAKING TIME: 1 HOUR
YIELD: 8 SERVINGS

3 cups pitted sweet cherries
3 eggs
⅓ cup honey
½ cup unbleached all-
  purpose flour
1¼ cups milk or light cream
2 tablespoons rum, kirsch, or
  Grand Marnier
1 tablespoon vanilla extract
½ teaspoon nutmeg
½ teaspoon cinnamon
1 tablespoon sugar

This is a traditional French dessert that resembles a puffy, baked fruit pancake.

Preheat the oven to 350° F.

Grease a 2-quart baking dish and lay the cherries on the bottom of the dish. In a medium-size mixing bowl, combine the eggs, honey, flour, milk, rum, and vanilla. Pour the custard over the fruit. Combine the remaining ingredients and sprinkle over the custard. Bake for 1 hour, or until the custard is set. Serve warm or cold.

Variations

Peach Clafouti. Use 3 cups peeled and sliced peaches in place of the cherries.

Pear Clafouti. Use 3 cups peeled and diced pears in place of the cherries.

Apple Clafouti. Sauté 3 cups apples in 3 tablespoons butter, ½ teaspoon cinnamon, and ¼ teaspoon cloves for 10 minutes. Then use this mixture in place of the cherries.

Raspberry Clafouti. Use 3 cups raspberries in place of the cherries.

Blueberry Clafouti. Use 3 cups blueberries in place of the cherries.

Steamed Pumpkin Pudding

PREPARATION TIME: 20 MINUTES
BAKING TIME: 1¼ HOURS
YIELD: 8 SERVINGS

1 cup pumpkin puree
(page 5)
⅔ cup buttermilk
⅓ cup butter, melted
2 eggs, beaten
½ cup honey
½ cup brown sugar, firmly
packed
1½ cups unbleached all-
purpose flour or ½ cup
whole wheat flour and 1
cup unbleached all-purpose
flour
2 teaspoons baking soda
1 teaspoon cinnamon
½ teaspoon nutmeg
½ teaspoon cloves
½ cup chopped walnuts
½ cup chopped dates

Preheat the oven to 350° F.

In a medium-size mixing bowl, combine the pumpkin, buttermilk, butter, eggs, honey, and brown sugar.

Sift together the flour, baking soda, cinnamon, nutmeg, and cloves. Add the dry ingredients to the pumpkin mixture and stir in the walnuts and dates. Pour the batter into a greased 9″ flan ring and cover with a double layer of aluminum foil. (You can substitute a 10″ tube pan if you don't have a flan ring.) Place the flan ring in a larger baking dish and pour in boiling water halfway up the side of the ring mold. Bake the pudding for 1¼ hours.

To unmold, place a serving dish upside down on top of the mold. Invert the mold and plate. The pudding will slip out of the mold.

Serve with whipped cream and Cider Sauce (page 145), if desired.

Variation

Steamed Winter Squash Pudding. Substitute 1 cup of pureed winter squash (page 5) for the pumpkin.

Four Treasure Rice Pudding With Pears

PREPARATION TIME: 20 MINUTES
BAKING TIME: 50 MINUTES
YIELD: 8 SERVINGS

3 cups cooked brown or
  white rice
1½ cups milk
3 eggs, separated
¼ cup butter, melted
½ cup honey, maple syrup,
  brown sugar, or white
  sugar
1 teaspoon vanilla extract
3 pears, peeled, cored, and
  diced to equal 1½ cups
  prepared fruit
¼ cup currants
¼ cup chopped dates
¼ cup chopped dried
  apricots
nutmeg as a garnish

Preheat the oven to 350° F.

In a medium-size saucepan, heat the rice with the milk over low heat and cook until the milk is completely absorbed.

Beat together the egg yolks, melted butter, sweetener, and vanilla. Blend the rice in with the egg mixture and add the fruits.

Beat the egg whites until stiff and fold them into the rice.

Grease a 2-quart baking dish and pour in the pudding. Sprinkle the top with nutmeg and bake for 50 minutes.

Serve warm with Cider Sauce (page 145) or Blueberry Orange Sauce (page 143) or Gingered Pear Sauce (Page 144).

Variations

Four Treasure Rice Pudding With Blueberries. Substitute 1½ cups blueberries for the pears. Serve with Blueberry Orange Sauce (page 143).

Four Treasure Rice Pudding With Peaches. Substitute 1½ cups peeled and diced peaches in place of the pears.

Four Treasure Rice Pudding With Berries. Substitute 1½ cups blackberries or raspberries in place of the pears.

Sweet Potato Maple Pudding

PREPARATION TIME: 20 MINUTES
BAKING TIME: 1 HOUR
YIELD: 10 SERVINGS

**3 cups grated raw sweet
  potatoes**
1 apple, chopped
½ cup maple syrup
4 eggs, beaten
4 tablespoons butter, melted
2 cups milk
1 teaspoon cinnamon
½ teaspoon salt
½ teaspoon nutmeg
½ teaspoon ground allspice
½ cup raisins
½ cup chopped almonds

Preheat the oven to 325° F.

Mix all the ingredients together and pour into a greased 2-quart baking dish. Bake for 1 hour, or until the custard is set. Serve warm with ice cream, if desired.

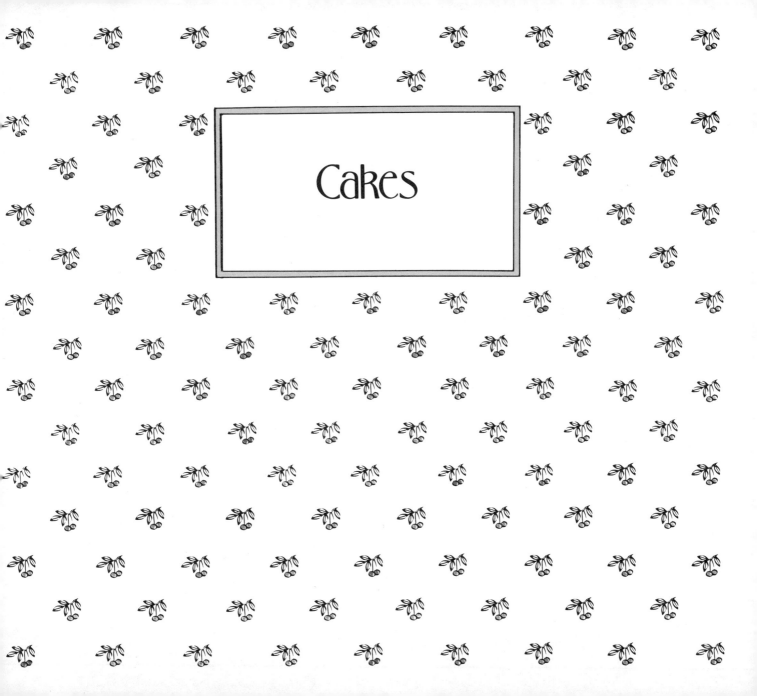

Cakes

Cakes are easy. They are also exacting. Follow a recipe to the letter and rarely will you have less than perfect cakes. Just assemble all your equipment and you are ready to create.

Choosing Your Baking Dishes

All of the recipes specify which size baking dish or pan to use. There is a reason for this. Most batters should be at least 1″ deep in the pan, or the cake will not rise properly. But if the pan is too small, the batter may overflow or the top may cave in. In most cake pans, the batter should fill the pan half to two-thirds full. Loaf pans and tube pans can be filled higher. Springform pans can be substituted for round cake pans. An 8″ × 8″ baking dish can be substituted for a 9″ round cake pan.

Preparing a Baking Pan

Cake pans should be greased with vegetable shortening, margarine, butter, or oil, and then dusted with flour. (I dust pans for chocolate cakes with cocoa.) If the recipe calls for the pan to be lined with waxed paper, grease the pan, then line with a piece of waxed paper cut to fit the pan exactly. Butter and flour the waxed paper. After the cake has been removed from the pan and cooled, peel off the waxed paper.

Loading the Oven

Before you begin to preheat the oven, make sure the oven racks are just above the center of the oven. There should be about 2″ in between pans to insure good heat circulation. Avoid placing the pans on separate racks.

Testing for Doneness

A cake is done when a toothpick or metal skewer inserted into the center of the cake comes out clean. If the cake is browning on top too quickly, but the cake is not yet done, you can cover the top loosely with aluminum foil or place a pan of water on the shelf above the cake and continue baking. This is especially likely to happen with cakes made with honey.

What Went Wrong?

Humped or cracked top
- Overmixing.
- Oven temperature too high.
- Batter not spread evenly in pan.
- Too much flour or not enough liquid.

One side higher
- Oven rack not level.
- Oven heat uneven.
- Batter not spread evenly.
- Pan warped.

Fallen center
- Oven temperature too low.
- Baking time too short.
- Not enough flour.
- Pan too small.

Soggy bottom layer
- Baking time too short.
- Undermixing.
- Too much liquid.

Hard top crust
- Oven temperature too high.
- Baking time too long.

Coarse texture
- Oven temperature too low.
- Undermixing.

Heavy, dense texture
- Oven temperature too high.
- Overmixing.
- Too much liquid or eggs.
- Not enough baking powder.

Deluxe Chocolate Cherry Cake

PREPARATION TIME: 30 MINUTES
BAKING TIME: 45 MINUTES
YIELD: 10 SERVINGS

Here's a variation on the classic Black Forest Cake. The cherry puree deepens the color of the chocolate and makes this cake especially moist.

Cake:

1½ cups unbleached all-
    purpose flour or ½ cup
    whole wheat flour and 1
    cup unbleached all-purpose
    flour
1 cup sugar
½ cup cocoa
1 teaspoon baking powder
1 teaspoon baking soda
½ teaspoon salt
2 cups sweet cherries, pitted
½ cup butter, melted
⅔ cup sour cream
3 eggs

Frosting:

2 cups whipping cream
½ cup confectioners' sugar
2 tablespoons kirsch or
  cherry juice

Preheat the oven to 350° F.

Sift together the flour, sugar, cocoa, baking powder, baking soda, and salt.

Puree 1 cup of the cherries in a blender or food processor. Cream together the butter, sour cream, eggs, and cherry puree. Add the dry ingredients and beat until smooth.

Butter and flour two 9″ round pans. Divide the batter between the pans. Sprinkle the remaining 1 cup of cherries over each cake and stir them gently into the batter. Bake for 45 minutes or until the cake tests done. Cool the cake completely before frosting.

Whip the frosting ingredients together until soft peaks form. Spread smoothly over the cake. Additional cherries can be used for decoration.

Pleasing Peach Cake

PREPARATION TIME: 20 MINUTES
BAKING TIME: 1 HOUR
YIELD: 8 SERVINGS

2 cups unbleached all-
   purpose flour or ¾ cup
   whole wheat flour and 1¼
   cups unbleached all-
   purpose flour
1 teaspoon baking powder
½ teaspoon baking soda
½ teaspoon salt
⅓ cup butter
⅔ cup honey
2 eggs
¼ cup yogurt
2 cups peeled and diced
   peaches (approximately 4
   peaches)
1 tablespoon grated lemon
   rind
½ cup chopped pecans
1 teaspoon vanilla extract
1 cup whipping cream
2–3 peaches, peeled and
   sliced

Preheat the oven to 350° F.

Sift together the flour, baking powder, baking soda, and salt. Set aside.

Cream the butter with the honey. Mix in the eggs and yogurt. Mix in the remaining ingredients, except the whipped cream and sliced peaches. Pour the batter into a greased 9″ × 5″ loaf pan and bake for 1 hour. Cool slightly.

Beat the cream and spread over the cake. Top with the sliced peaches and serve.

Andrea's Green Tomato Chocolate Cake

PREPARATION TIME: 30 MINUTES
BAKING TIME: 35 MINUTES
YIELD: 12–15 SERVINGS

⅔ cup butter
1¾ cups sugar
4 ounces unsweetened
   chocolate, melted
2 eggs
1 teaspoon vanilla extract
½ cup cocoa
2½ cups unbleached all-
   purpose flour or 1½ cups
   unbleached all-purpose
   flour and 1 cup whole
   wheat flour
2 teaspoons baking powder
2 teaspoons baking soda
¼ teaspoon salt
1 cup beer
1 cup pureed raw green
   tomatoes
¼–½ cup water (optional)

This recipe first appeared in Garden Way's Red and Green Tomato Cookbook. *It is such a great cake, I adapted it for zucchini, too.*

Preheat the oven to 350° F.

Cream together the butter and sugar. Stir in the melted chocolate, then the eggs, one at a time. Add the vanilla.

In another bowl, sift together the cocoa, flour, baking powder, baking soda, and salt.

Add the flour mixture to the butter mixture alternately with the beer and green tomatoes. If the batter appears very stiff, add the water. (Sometimes the moisture content of the tomatoes varies.)

Turn the batter into 2 greased and floured 9″ cake pans. Bake for 35 minutes. Cool. Frost with Cream Cheese Frosting (page 68) or whipped cream, or serve plain. This is a very rich, moist cake.

Variation

Janet's Zucchini Chocolate Cake. Substitute 1 cup of zucchini, grated and drained, for the pureed green tomatoes.

Sweetheart Beet Cake

PREPARATION TIME: 30 MINUTES
BAKING TIME: 30 MINUTES
YIELD: 12 SERVINGS

This makes a very pretty 3-layer cake. It can be made with canned, but not pickled, beets.

Cake:

3 cups unbleached all-
    purpose flour
3½ teaspoons baking powder
1 teaspoon salt
⅔ cup butter at room
    temperature
2 cups sugar
4 eggs
1¼ cups pureed cooked beets
    (page 4)
1 teaspoon vanilla extract

Frosting:

2 cups whipping cream
½ cup confectioners' sugar
1 teaspoon vanilla extract

Preheat the oven to 350° F.

Sift together the flour, baking powder, and salt. In a medium-size mixing bowl, cream the butter and 2 cups sugar together until thoroughly mixed. Beat in the eggs, one at a time. Stir in the pureed cooked beets and 1 teaspoon vanilla. Stir in the dry ingredients.

Butter and flour three 9″ cake pans. Divide the batter between the 3 pans and place on the middle rack of the oven. Bake for 30 minutes, or until the cake tests done. Remove the cake from the pans and allow to cool completely.

To make the frosting, beat the cream and sweeten with the confectioners' sugar and 1 teaspoon vanilla. Frost the cooled cake.

Rhubarb Sour Cream Cake

PREPARATION TIME: 20 MINUTES
BAKING TIME: 40 MINUTES
YIELD: 10 SERVINGS

The rhubarb in this cake needs no precooking, which makes the preparation time brief. This recipe is easily doubled or tripled to serve a crowd.

Cake:

¼ cup butter at room temperature
1½ cups brown sugar, packed
2 large eggs
1 teaspoon vanilla extract
2⅓ cups unbleached all-purpose flour or 2 cups unbleached all-purpose flour and ½ cup wheat germ
1 teaspoon baking soda
1 teaspoon salt
1 pound rhubarb, cut in ½" pieces (4 cups)
1 cup sour cream

Topping:

½ cup sugar
1 teaspoon cinnamon
1 cup chopped nuts

Preheat the oven to 350° F.

Cream the butter and sugar until fluffy. Beat in the eggs and vanilla.

Sift together the flour, baking soda, and salt. Add to the butter mixture. Add the rhubarb and sour cream. Blend well. The batter will be thick. Grease a 9" × 13" baking pan and pour the batter into the pan.

Combine the topping ingredients. Sprinkle on top of the batter.

Bake for 40 minutes, or until the top springs back when pressed, or a toothpick, inserted, comes out clean. Serve warm with whipped cream spooned on top.

Cherry Sour Cream Honey Cake

PREPARATION TIME: 30 MINUTES
BAKING TIME: 30–40 MINUTES
YIELD: 12 SERVINGS

1 cup butter at room
   temperature
2 cups honey
2 teaspoons vanilla extract
6 eggs
1½ cups unbleached all-
   purpose flour
1½ cups whole wheat flour
¼ teaspoon baking soda
½ teaspoon salt
1 cup sour cream
2 cups sour cherries, pitted
grated rind from 1 lemon

Preheat the oven to 350° F.

Cream together the butter and the honey until the mixture is light. Add the vanilla and eggs.

Sift together the dry ingredients. Add them to the butter mixture. Add the sour cream. Mix well until the batter is blended. Mix in the sour cherries and lemon rind.

Grease a 10″ tube pan. Spoon in the batter. Bake the cake for 30–40 minutes or until the cake pulls away from the side of the pan. Cool the cake for 10 minutes, then invert it onto a cake plate. Serve with whipped cream and Sour Cherry Sauce (page 143).

Variations

Sweet Potato Honey Cake. Replace the cherries with 2 cups grated raw sweet potatoes.

Zucchini Honey Cake. Replace the cherries with 2 cups grated raw zucchini.

Green Tomato Honey Cake. Finely chop 2–3 large green tomatoes. In a medium-size saucepan, combine 2 cups chopped green tomatoes with ¼ cup brown sugar, ½ teaspoon cinnamon, and 1 tablespoon lemon juice. Gently simmer for 5 minutes. Drain the tomatoes and stir into the batter in place of the cherries.

Blueberry Honey Cake. Substitute 2 cups blueberries for the cherries.

Blackberry Honey Cake. Substitute 2 cups blackberries for the cherries.

Raspberry Honey Cake. Substitute 2 cups raspberries for the cherries.

Apple Spice Cake Roll

PREPARATION TIME: 20 MINUTES
BAKING TIME: 20 MINUTES
YIELD: 8–10 SERVINGS

Cake:

3 eggs
¾ cup white sugar or ½ cup honey
½ cup apple sauce or puree (page 4)
½ cup raisins or currants
1 cup unbleached all-purpose flour or ½ cup whole wheat flour and ½ cup unbleached all-purpose flour
½ teaspoon baking powder
½ teaspoon baking soda
1 teaspoon cinnamon
¼ teaspoon salt
¼ teaspoon allspice
¼ teaspoon cloves

Filling:

8 ounces cream cheese at room temperature
¼ cup apple sauce or puree (page 4)
2 tablespoons brown sugar
confectioners' sugar for dusting

Preheat the oven to 375° F.

In a medium-size mixing bowl, beat the eggs until they are light yellow. Add the sugar and continue beating until this mixture is thick, about 5–8 minutes. Fold in ½ cup apple sauce and the raisins.

Sift together the dry ingredients and fold them gently into the batter.

Grease the bottom of a 15½" × 10½" × 1" jelly roll pan and fit with waxed paper. Grease and flour the paper. Pour the batter onto the waxed paper and spread it evenly to the edges. Bake the cake for 15–20 minutes.

While the cake bakes, blend together the cream cheese, apple sauce, and sugar in a mixer.

When the cake is done, remove it from the oven and immediately turn it onto a tea towel that has been dusted with confectioners' sugar. Remove the waxed paper. Roll the cake up in the towel and allow it to cool for 10 minutes. Then unroll the cake and spread it with the cream cheese filling. Reroll the cake. Chill well before serving. Garnish with whipped cream if desired.

Variations

Strawberry Roll. Substitute ½ cup strawberry puree (page 5) for the apple sauce in the batter and omit the spices and raisins. Substitute ¼ cup strawberry puree for the apple sauce in the filling and increase the sugar by 2 tablespoons. Sprinkle 1 cup of strawberry pieces over the cream cheese before you roll the cake up. Chill and serve.

Apple Butter Cake Roll. Substitute ¼ cup apple butter for ¼ cup apple sauce in the filling. *Or,* substitute ½ cup apple butter for the cream cheese and apple sauce filling.

Apple Gingerbread Upside-Down Cake

PREPARATION TIME: 20 MINUTES
BAKING TIME: 45 MINUTES
YIELD: 8–10 SERVINGS

11 tablespoons butter
1 cup brown sugar
4 large tart apples, peeled
   and sliced
2 cups unbleached all-
   purpose flour or 1 cup
   whole wheat flour and 1
   cup unbleached all-purpose
   flour
1 teaspoon baking powder
1 teaspoon baking soda
½ teaspoon salt
1½ teaspoons cinnamon
1 teaspoon ginger
1 teaspoon cardamom
½ teaspoon cloves
2 eggs
1 cup molasses
1 cup buttermilk

Preheat the oven to 375° F.

Melt 3 tablespoons of butter in a 9″ round cake pan or 9″ spring-form pan and mix in ½ cup brown sugar. Remove the pan from the heat and arrange the apples over the bottom of the pan.

Sift together the flour, baking powder, baking soda, salt, and spices. Cream the remaining ½ cup butter with the remaining ½ cup brown sugar. Add the eggs. Alternately add the dry ingredients and the molasses and buttermilk to the sugar mixture, mixing well after each addition. Pour the batter over the apples and bake for 45 minutes or until the cake tests done. Allow the cake to cool for 45 minutes. Place a serving platter upside down on top of the cake pan. Invert the plate and pan at once to invert the cake. Remove the pan and serve the cake with whipped cream or ice cream, if desired.

Variations

Pear Upside-Down Cake. Replace the apples with 4–5 large pears, peeled and sliced. Sprinkle ½ cup raisins over the pears before pouring on the batter.

Peach Upside-Down Cake. Replace the apples with 5–6 large peaches, peeled and sliced.

Parsnip Spice Cake

PREPARATION TIME: 20 MINUTES
BAKING TIME: 1 HOUR
YIELD: 10–12 SERVINGS

2 cups unbleached all-
  purpose flour or ¾ cup
  whole wheat flour and 1¼
  cups unbleached all-
  purpose flour
2 cups sugar
2 teaspoons baking powder
2 teaspoons baking soda
1 teaspoon salt
1 tablespoon cinnamon
1 teaspoon nutmeg
5 eggs
1¼ cups vegetable oil
3 cups grated raw parsnips
2 teaspoons vanilla extract
1 teaspoon grated lemon rind
1 cup walnuts
3½ cups Cream Cheese
  Frosting (page 68)

Preheat the oven to 350° F.

Sift together the flour, sugar, baking powder, baking soda, salt, cinnamon, and nutmeg. In a large mixing bowl, beat the eggs slightly. Add the oil, parsnips, vanilla, lemon rind, and walnuts. Stir in the dry ingredients and mix well.

Grease a 9″ × 13″ pan or a 10″ tube pan. Pour the batter into the pan and bake for 1 hour. Cool completely and frost with Cream Cheese Frosting.

Variations

Zucchini Apple Spice Cake. Use 2 cups grated raw zucchini and 1 cup grated peeled apple in place of the parsnips.

Carrot Spice Cake. Use 3 cups grated carrots, ½ cup raisins, and ½ cup pineapple chunks in place of the parsnips.

Sweet Potato Spice Cake. Use 3 cups grated raw sweet potato in place of the parsnips.

Pumpkin or Hubbard Squash Spice Cake. Use 3 cups grated raw pumpkin or squash in place of the parsnips.

Pumpkin Puree Spice Cake. Substitute 2 cups pureed pumpkin (page 5) for the parsnips. Increase the flour to 3 cups. Bake the cake for 1¼ hours.

Quick Peach Kuchen

PREPARATION TIME: 30 MINUTES
BAKING TIME: 40 MINUTES
YIELD: 10–12 SERVINGS

This is a delicious cake that uses both baking powder and yeast, but has no rising time, so it's perfect to make when time is short. The kuchen is equally delicious with any fruit you have on hand—peaches, apples, pears, or berries.

Kuchen:

½ tablespoon active dry yeast

2 tablespoons warm water

1 teaspoon plus ½ cup sugar

2 cups unbleached all-purpose flour or ½ cup whole wheat and 1½ cups unbleached all-purpose flour

1 tablespoon baking powder

½ teaspoon salt

½ cup butter at room temperature

2 eggs

grated rind from 1 lemon

¼ teaspoon lemon extract

¼ cup milk

2½ cups peeled and sliced peaches

Preheat the oven to 350° F.

In a small bowl, mix the yeast, warm water, and 1 teaspoon sugar together, and set aside.

Sift together the flour, baking powder, and salt.

In a mixing bowl, cream the butter and the remaining ½ cup sugar together until the mixture is light and lemon colored. Add the eggs, grated lemon rind, lemon extract, add yeast mixture. Continue beating. Mix in the flour and the milk and beat for 3 minutes more.

Butter a 9″ × 13″ baking dish. Spread half the batter into the pan. Arrange the fruit slices on top. Drop the remaining dough on top of the fruit. Mix together the topping ingredients and sprinkle over the cake. Bake for 40 minutes.

Topping:

½ cup firmly packed brown
   sugar
¼ cup unbleached all-
   purpose flour
1 teaspoon cinnamon
3 tablespoons butter
½ cup chopped almonds

Variations

Quick Apple Kuchen. Substitute 2½ cups peeled and sliced apples for the peaches.

Quick Blueberry Kuchen. Substitute 2½ cups blueberries for the peaches.

Quick Pear Kuchen. Substitute 2½ cups peeled and sliced pears for the peaches.

Carrot Almond Torte

PREPARATION TIME: 30 MINUTES
BAKING TIME: 1 HOUR
YIELD: 12 SERVINGS

Cake:

8 eggs, separated
2 cups sugar
1 tablespoon lemon juice
rind of 1 lemon, grated
½ teaspoon almond extract
1 teaspoon vanilla extract
2 cups grated carrots, firmly
   packed
2 cups almonds, blanched
   and finely ground

Frosting:

1½ cups whipping cream
½ cup confectioners' sugar
½ teaspoon almond extract
1 cup slivered almonds

Tortes are cakes made with either ground nuts or bread crumbs instead of flour. They are richer than flour cakes. This torte is particularly moist. Store it in the refrigerator if you don't eat it all in a day.

Preheat the oven to 350° F.

In a medium-size mixing bowl, beat together the egg yolks and sugar until thick and lemon colored. Mix in the lemon juice, lemon rind, and the vanilla and almond extracts.

Steam the carrots for 5 minutes until soft, and rinse in cold water to cool. Pat dry and stir the grated carrots and ground almonds into the egg mixture.

Beat the egg whites until stiff and fold into the carrot batter. Grease and flour two 9″ cake pans and divide the batter between them. Bake for 1 hour. Cool the cake completely.

Beat the cream with the confectioners' sugar and almond extract. Frost the cake with the whipped cream and decorate the sides of the cake with the slivered almonds.

Raspberry Nut Cake

PREPARATION TIME: 20 MINUTES
BAKING TIME: 40 MINUTES
YIELD: 10 SERVINGS

Cake:

½ cup butter
1 cup brown sugar, firmly
   packed
3 eggs
¾ cup sour cream
1 teaspoon vanilla extract
1 teaspoon almond extract
2 cups all-purpose unbleached
   flour, or 1 cup whole
   wheat flour and 1 cup
   unbleached all-purpose
   flour
1½ teaspoons baking
   powder
½ teaspoon baking soda
½ teaspoon salt
½ cup chopped almonds
1 cup fresh raspberries

Preheat the oven to 350° F.

In a medium-size mixing bowl, cream together the butter and brown sugar. Add the eggs and beat well. Mix in the sour cream and vanilla and almond extracts.

Sift together the flour, baking powder, baking soda, and salt. Add the dry ingredients to the butter and sugar mixture and mix well. Stir in the nuts and raspberries. Grease a 9″ × 13″ pan and pour in the batter. Bake for 40 minutes or until the cake tests done. Cool before frosting.

Frosting:

2 tablespoons butter

¼ teaspoon almond extract

1 tablespoon raspberry puree or jam

1 tablespoon cream

1½ cups confectioners' sugar

To make the frosting, cream the butter with the almond extract, raspberry puree, and cream. Blend in the confectioners' sugar. Add more confectioners' sugar if necessary to make a stiff frosting. Spread on top of the cooled cake and allow the frosting to set for at least 15 minutes before serving.

Chocolate Sauerkraut Cake

PREPARATION TIME: 20 MINUTES
BAKING TIME: 35 MINUTES
YIELD: 10–12 SERVINGS

This is a great conversation cake! The sauerkraut has a texture like coconut when it is baked.

⅔ cup butter at room temperature

1½ cups sugar

3 eggs

1 teaspoon vanilla extract

2½ cups unbleached all-purpose flour

1 teaspoon baking powder

1 teaspoon baking soda

¼ teaspoon salt

½ cup cocoa

1 cup water

1 cup sauerkraut, minced finely

Preheat the oven to 350° F.

Cream together the butter and sugar. Add the eggs, one at a time. Mix in the vanilla.

Sift together the flour, baking powder, baking soda, salt, and cocoa. Add a third of the flour mixture and a third of the water to the butter and sugar. Mix until blended. Continue adding the flour and water alternately, until the batter is well blended.

Rinse the sauerkraut and squeeze out the excess water and juice. Stir the sauerkraut into the cake batter.

Butter and flour two 9″ round cake pans. Pour half the batter into each prepared cake pan. Bake the cake for 35 minutes or until the cake tests done. Allow the cake to cool. Then frost with Cream Cheese Frosting (page 68) or whipped cream.

Cardamom Apple Sauce Cake With Sour Cream Topping

PREPARATION TIME: 20 MINUTES
BAKING TIME: 50 MINUTES
YIELD: 8–10 SERVINGS

Cake:

1¾ cups unbleached all-
   purpose flour or ¾ cup
   whole wheat flour and 1
   cup unbleached all-purpose
   flour
½ teaspoon salt
1 teaspoon baking soda
1 teaspoon cinnamon
½ teaspoon cloves
½ teaspoon cardamom
1 teaspoon ginger
½ cup butter at room
   temperature
1 cup sugar
1 egg
1 cup apple sauce or apple
   puree (page 4)
½ cup raisins
½ cup chopped walnuts

Preheat the oven to 350° F.

Sift together the flour, salt, baking soda, and spices. Set aside.

Cream together the butter and sugar, beating until the mixture is light and fluffy. Beat in 1 cup apple sauce. Add the flour mixture and stir until well blended. Add the raisins and nuts. Pour the batter into a greased 9″ × 13″ baking dish. Bake for 30 minutes.

To make the topping, combine the 1 cup apple sauce with 1 tablespoon brown sugar and ½ teaspoon cinnamon. Remove the cake from the oven and spread the topping mixture over it.

Mix together the sour cream, the remaining 2 tablespoons brown sugar, and the vanilla. Carefully spread the sour cream mixture over the apple sauce. Return the cake to the oven and bake for an additional 20 minutes.

Topping:

1 cup apple sauce or apple puree (page 4)
3 tablespoons brown sugar
½ teaspoon cinnamon
½ cup sour cream
½ teaspoon vanilla extract

Variation

Cardamom Apple Sauce Cake With Apple Cider Icing. Make the Apple Sauce Cake as above, but do not make the topping. Bake the cake for 50 minutes, then cool. To make the frosting, combine ¾ teaspoon cinnamon and 2 tablespoons apple cider with 1 cup confectioners' sugar. Blend until smooth. Add more confectioners' sugar if needed to thicken the frosting. Spread over the cooled cake. Allow the frosting to set for at least 15 minutes before serving.

Candied Mint Leaves and Violets

Use candied mint leaves and candied violets to decorate cakes and fruit compotes.

Collect unblemished mint leaves or violets from your garden. Wash and dry them. Beat together 1 egg white and 1 tablespoon lemon juice until slightly frothy. With a small paint brush, paint the leaves and flowers with this mixture. Gently sprinkle each leaf and flower with superfine sugar, until they are coated. Lay the leaves and flowers on waxed paper. Allow them to dry on one side (1 hour). Then turn them over so they can dry on the other side. They keep well in airtight jars.

Rose Geranium Sugar

PREPARATION TIME: 5 MINUTES
WAITING TIME: 3 DAYS
YIELD: 4 CUPS

4 cups granulated sugar
8 rose geranium leaves,
   finely diced

Rose Geranium Sugar can be used in place of granulated sugar in any cake or cookie or frosting recipe for a delightful change in flavor. Or use it to sweeten your fruit.

Combine the sugar and leaves and mix well. Place in a covered container and let it rest for 3 days. Sift out the leaves, if desired, and use the sugar anytime.

Cream Cheese Frosting

PREPARATION TIME: 10–15
   MINUTES
YIELD: 3½ CUPS

8 ounces cream cheese at
   room temperature
¾ cup butter at room
   temperature
4 cups confectioners' sugar

This recipe makes enough frosting to cover a 2-layer or 3-layer 9" cake.

Cream together the cream cheese and butter. Slowly add the confectioners' sugar and beat until smooth. If the frosting is too thin, add more sugar.

Pies, Tarts, and Flans

What makes a pastry crust flaky? When tiny, cold lumps of fat in the dough are heated rapidly, they explode, creating miniature air pockets. Understanding this, you can see that the dough should be cold when it goes into the oven, and that the pastry should be handled lightly so that your hands do not crush or warm the fat particles. That's all there is to it.

You will find recipes for various pie and tart crusts on pages 79–86, and various fillings throughout the rest of the chapter. Here are a few pointers.

Measure your fat exactly. Too much fat makes the dough greasy and crumbly.

Cut the fat into the flour and salt mixture with a pastry cutter or 2 knives until the texture resembles peas and cornmeal.

Add the water slowly. Because flour absorbs moisture from the air, it is impossible to determine exactly how much water should be added. Add the water 1 tablespoon at a time. Push the moistened dough to one side, and add more water, again a tablespoon at a time. If you dump all the water in at one time, or allow the water to sit in the flour and fat mixture, the dough will absorb more water than is necessary, so stir immediately. Too much water makes a crust hard and brittle.

Handle the dough lightly to avoid warming or crushing the fat and to prevent gluten from developing, which will make the crust tough. Also, a light touch incorporates air in the dough, which contributes to its flakiness.

Form the dough into a ball and refrigerate until you are ready to use it. This tenderizes the dough, prevents shrinking in the pan, and makes it easier to handle.

Always preheat the oven.

Nonshiny pie pans are best for even browning of the crust, which is why I prefer glass pie pans.

Buttering the pan will brown the bottom crust, a good idea with fruit pies.

Roll out the dough on a lightly floured surface. Slightly flatten the dough ball with the heel of your hand. Always roll from the center of the dough to the edges. Lift the rolling pin and return to the center. Roll evenly and smoothly, until the dough is ⅛″ thick. Trim the dough so that it is 2″ larger than the pie pan.

To lift the crust into the pie pan, loosen the dough from the board. Loosely roll the crust onto the rolling pin, center over the pie pan, and unroll. Or fold the dough in half and carefully lift onto the pie pan and unfold. Ease the crust into the pan and fit into place so no air pockets are left between the pan and crust.

To bake a crust without filling (the English call this baking "blind"), prick holes in the crust to release air and prevent the crust from humping. Or, weight the crust with dried beans or clean pebbles on a piece of waxed paper. Remove the weights a few minutes before the baking time is up.

If your fruit pies tend to bubble over, place aluminum foil on the bottom of the oven to catch the drips. Never set your pie on a baking sheet as this interferes with the browning of the crust.

If your fruit pies tend to have soggy bottom crusts, brush the bottom crust with egg white before spooning in the filling. If possible, the filling should be hot when spooned into the shell.

If the edges of the pie are browning too rapidly, cover the edges with a strip of aluminum foil. You can also remove the center from a 10″ disposable pie pan. The 2″ ring that remains can be placed upside down on a 9″ pie pan while the pie bakes to slow the browning. Save the pie ring to use again.

Fruit pies will run less and will look more attractive when served if you allow the pie to cool for at least 30 minutes before serving.

Lining a Tart Pan or Springform Pan With Dough

Shape the dough into a ball and flatten it to make a circle about 1½″ thick. On a lightly floured surface, roll out the dough, working from the center to the edges to form a circle of dough that is ⅛–¼″ thick. The circle should be a little larger than the pan. Loosely roll the dough onto the rolling pin and unroll it on the pan. Gently press the dough into the pan and against the sides. If you are using a fluted tart pan, be sure to press the pastry against the fluted edges. Using the rolling pin, roll over the top of the tart pan to cut away excess dough. Cut away any excess dough inside the springform pan.

If you are prebaking the pastry before it is filled, prick the dough all over the bottom with a fork and bake for 15 minutes. Alternatively, you could weight the crust with dried beans or clean pebbles on a piece of waxed paper. Bake the crust for 20 minutes. Remove the weights a few minutes before the baking time is up. The weight of the beans will prevent the crust from puffing up. Cool the crust and fill with the desired filling.

Final Touches for Pastry Crusts

The top crust of your filled pies can be decoratively varied with lattice tops, or a solid crust can be glazed or carved. Here's how.

Lattice Tops

Roll out the dough slightly thicker than normal to make it easier to handle. It is easiest to make the lattice directly on the pie. But you will have cleaner results if you lay out the lattice on a cookie sheet and then slide the lattice onto the filled pie.

Simple Lattice. Line the pan with the bottom crust, leaving a 1″ overhang. Spoon in the filling. Roll out the top crust to make a circle of dough slightly larger than the pie pan. Cut the dough into ½″ strips. Moisten the rim of the bottom crust with water.

Lay half of the strips over the pie about 1″ apart. Lay the remaining strips over the pie about 1″ apart in the opposite direction to form either a diamond or a simple square pattern. Trim the strips flush with the outside pie edge. Turn the overhanging bottom crust up over the rim of the pie pan and the ends of the strips. Press firmly all around to seal the strips to the rim. Flute the edges.

Woven Lattice. Line the pie pan with the bottom crust, leaving a 1″ overhang. Spoon in the filling. Roll out the top crust to make a circle of dough slightly larger than the pie pan. Cut the dough into ½″ strips. Moisten the rim of the bottom crust with water.

Lay half of the strips over the pie, about 1″ apart. Fold back every other strip, partially exposing the center of the pie. Lay a strip of dough across the center of the pie. Unfold the strips. Fold back the strips you did not fold back originally. Lay another strip about 1″ from the center strip. Unfold the strips. Continue, folding alternate strips and laying strips 1″ apart until the weaving is completed on one side. Work from the center to the edges of the other side.

woven lattice

Trim the strips flush with the outside pie edge. Turn the overhanging bottom crust up over the rim and ends of the strips. Press firmly all around to seal the strips to the rim. Flute the edges.

Spiral Topping. Line the pan with the bottom crust, leaving a 1" overhang. Spoon in the filling. Roll out the top crust to make a circle of dough. Cut the dough into strips ¾" wide and fasten the strips into a single long strip by moistening the ends with water and pressing with your fingers.

Starting from the center of the pie, twist and spiral the dough moving from the center to the outer edge. Cut the spiral end off flush with the outside edge of the pie pan. Turn the overhanging bottom crust up over the rim and the end of the spiral strip. Press firmly to seal the spiral to the rim. Flute the edges.

Victory Top. Line the pan with the bottom crust, leaving a 1" overhang. Spoon in the filling. Roll out the top crust to make a circle of dough slightly larger than the pie pan. Cut the dough into ½" strips. Moisten the rim of the bottom crust with water.

Arrange 4 long strips over the top of the pie to bisect the pie into 8 even sections. These strips outline the pieces to be cut from the pie (the cutting line will be beside the pastry strips). Use the remaining pastry strips to make 2 smaller V shapes inside each of the larger wedges. Trim the edges of the strips flush with the outside pie edge. Turn the overhanging bottom crust up over the rim of the pie pan and the ends of the strips. Press firmly all around to seal the strips to the rim. Flute the edges.

Decorated Solid Tops

To make a solid top, roll the dough out 1" larger than your pie pan. As the pie bakes, steam will form and must be released. You can make a few simple gashes in the top crust or prick steam holes with your fork, to allow steam to escape. Or you can incorporate the steam vents into a carved design.

victory top

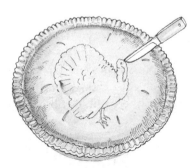
picture top

Initial Tops. Cut initials with a knife or prick with your fork. The initials can represent the person who will be receiving the pie, or the first letter of the pie filling: A for apple, B for blueberry. These initials are useful at bake sales to identify the filling.

Picture Tops. If you are handy with a knife, outline a picture commemorating the holiday or meal—a turkey for Thanksgiving, for example.

Then roll half the dough onto your rolling pin and lift it onto the filled pie, centering the crust over the pie. Unroll the dough. Trim the pastry ½″ beyond the rim and fold the top crust up over the bottom crust. Now you are ready to flute the edges.

Decorating the Edges

No pie is finished without a decorative edge. Here's a sampling of easy flutes to try.

Simple Flute. Place your left index finger facing the outside of the rim of the pastry. With your right thumb and index finger on the outside of the pastry, press the pastry into V shapes, working your way around the rim, pressing every ½″. Pinch the raised flutes to make sharp points.

Scallops. Form the edges like flutes, but do not press into points. Flatten the top of each flute with a 4-tined fork.

Fork Trim. Fold under the overhanging pastry and press the rim to form a high standing edge. At ½″ intervals, press down the pastry with a 4-tined fork.

Rope Trim. Fold under the overhanging pastry and press the rim to form a high standing edge. Press the side of your right thumb into the pastry. With the knuckle of your index finger, pinch the pastry

simple flute

fork trim

between your thumb and knuckle. Repeat the pattern at ½″ intervals all around the pie.

Coin Trim. Trim the pastry even with the edge of the pie pan. With the remaining pastry scraps, cut circles of dough using a bottle cap dipped in flour. Moisten the edge of the pie with cold water. Place the dough circles around the edge of the pastry, overlapping them slightly. Press the dough lightly into the rim of the pie pan.

Fluted Coin. Fold under the overhanging pastry and press the rim to form a high standing edge. Flute the edges. From the extra pastry, cut rounds of dough to a size that will fit the indentation of fluting. Moisten the outside edges of the fluting and press a dough round into each indentation standing on its edge.

Wreath. Fold under the overhanging pastry and press the rim to form a high standing edge. Snip the pastry with scissors at ½″ intervals. Lay the cut pieces alternately toward the pie and away from the pie.

wreath

Ruffles. Fold the overhanging pastry on the edge of the pan loosely. Slip your left index finger under the fold of pastry. Press your right index finger firmly next to the lifted pastry to make a ruffle. Continue all around the pan.

Button. Fold under the overhanging pastry. Use the handle end of a measuring spoon to press a design into the edge. The hole in the end of the spoon makes a button design.

Glazing the Top

For a shiny top, before the pie goes into the oven, brush the crust with a slightly beaten egg or with just the white or yellow part of an

ruffles

egg, if you have leftovers. Or, 15 minutes before the baking time is up, brush the crust with cream, milk, melted butter or margarine, or salad oil.

For a sparkling top, moisten the top crust with water and sprinkle with sugar or sugar and cinnamon.

What Went Wrong?

Pie crust is tough
- Not enough fat.
- Too much flour; probably your rolling surface was too heavily floured.
- Overhandled or rerolled the crust.
- Too much water was added.

Pie crust is too crumbly
- Too much fat.
- Not enough water.
- Water and fat were not evenly distributed in the crust.

Pie crust shrank
- The dough was stretched when it was fitted into the pan.
- Not enough steam holes were made.
- The dough was rolled unevenly or patched together.

Pie crust was soggy
- The pie was not baked long enough.
- The oven temperature was too low.
- There was a tear in the bottom crust.
- There was a long wait before the filled crust was placed in the oven.

Single Crust Pastry

PREPARATION TIME: 15 MINUTES
BAKING TIME: 10–15 MINUTES
YIELD: 1 SINGLE 9″ or
   10″ BOTTOM CRUST

1 cup unbleached all-purpose
   flour
½ teaspoon salt
⅓ cup butter, shortening,
   margarine, or lard
2–2½ tablespoons cold water

In a medium-size bowl, mix the flour and salt. Cut the butter or shortening into the flour with a pastry blender, 2 knives, or your fingers (working quickly) until the mixture resembles peas and cornmeal. Sprinkle the water lightly into the dough as it comes together in a ball. Refrigerate for at least 1 hour or until you are ready to use the pastry.

On a lightly floured surface, roll out the crust, gently working from the center out in all directions until you make a 12″ circle and the dough is ⅛″ thick.

Fold the rolled dough in half and ease it carefully into a pie pan with the fold in the center. Unfold the dough and press out the air pockets. Repair any holes or openings in the crust. Trim the dough to 1″ beyond the edge of the pie pan. Fold under the edge. Crimp the edge in a decorative style (see pages 76–77). Fill the pie shell and bake according to the specific recipe directions.

To bake unfilled, prick the dough with a fork, covering the surface of the pie shell with tiny holes that will allow steam to escape. Bake in a 450° F. oven for 10–15 minutes or until browned.

Basic Double Crust Pastry

PREPARATION TIME: 15 MINUTES
BAKING TIME: ACCORDING TO
 SPECIFIC RECIPE
 INSTRUCTIONS
YIELD: TOP AND BOTTOM PIE
 CRUST

**2 cups unbleached all-
 purpose flour**
1 teaspoon salt
**⅔ cup butter, margarine,
 shortening, lard**
6–7 tablespoons cold water

In a medium-size bowl, mix together the flour and salt. Cut the butter or shortening into the flour with a pastry blender, 2 knives, or your fingers (working quickly), until the mixture resembles peas and cornmeal. Sprinkle the water over the flour and blend lightly into the dough as it forms a ball. Cut the ball in half and refrigerate for at least 1 hour or until you are ready to use it.

On a lightly floured surface, slightly flatten one dough ball.

Roll out the crust, gently working from the center out in all directions until you have a 12″ circle and the dough is ⅛″ thick.

Fold the rolled dough in half and ease it carefully into a pie pan with the fold in the center. Unfold the dough and trim the crust to the edge of the pie pan. Pour your filling into the crust and brush the edge of the crust with water.

Roll out the top crust in the same manner, but make a slightly larger circle. Trim the crust ½″ beyond the edge of the pie plate. Fold the extra pastry under the bottom crust. Crimp the edges (see pages 76–77). Brush the crust with a beaten egg and pierce in several places to allow steam to escape.

Bake as directed according to the individual recipe.

Whole Wheat Single Pie Crust

PREPARATION TIME: 15 MINUTES
BAKING TIME: 10–15 MINUTES
YIELD: 1 SINGLE 9″ or
   10″ BOTTOM CRUST

1¼ cups whole wheat flour
½ teaspoon salt
6 tablespoons butter or solid
   vegetable shortening
2–3 tablespoons water

In a medium-size mixing bowl, combine the flour and the salt. Cut in the butter until the mixture resembles gravel or coarse sand. Add the water and mix just enough to bring the dough together. Form the dough into a ball. Do not handle too much. Refrigerate for at least 1 hour or until you are ready to use it. Turn the dough onto a lightly floured board, flatten the ball, and roll it out into a 12″ circle. This is a crumbly pie dough and it requires extra care when rolling it out. Patch any tears or holes as they appear.

Lift the dough carefully into a pie pan by rolling half the dough onto your rolling pin, then unrolling the dough into the pan. Cut and crimp the edges. Fill the pie shell and bake according to the specific recipe directions.

To bake unfilled, prick the dough with a fork, covering the surface of the pie shell with tiny holes that will allow steam to escape. Bake in a 450° oven for 10–15 minutes or until browned.

Variation

Whole Wheat Double Pie Crust. Use 2 cups whole wheat flour, ¾ teaspoon salt, ½ cup butter or solid vegetable shortening, and 4 tablespoons water. Proceed as above, and bake according to the individual recipe directions.

Half and Half Single Pie Crust

PREPARATION TIME: 15 MINUTES
BAKING TIME: 10–15 MINUTES
YIELD: 1 SINGLE 9″ OR
  10″ BOTTOM CRUST

This pie dough is a little easier to handle than the Whole Wheat Pie Crust.

½ cup whole wheat flour
¾ cup unbleached all-
  purpose flour
½ teaspoon salt
6 tablespoons butter or solid
  vegetable shortening
2–3 tablespoons cold water

In a medium-size mixing bowl, combine the flours and salt. Cut in the butter until the mixture resembles gravel or coarse sand. Add the water and mix the dough just enough to form a ball. Refrigerate for at least one hour or until you are ready to use the pastry.

Turn the dough out onto a lightly floured board, flatten the ball, and roll out to form a 12″ circle. Lift the dough by loosely rolling half of it onto your rolling pin and fit the crust into the pie pan. Cut and crimp the edges. Fill the pie shell and bake according to specific recipe directions.

To bake unfilled, prick the dough with a fork, covering the surface of the pie shell with tiny holes that will allow steam to escape. Bake in a 450° oven for 10–15 minutes or until browned.

Variation

Half and Half Double Pie Crust. Use ¾ cup whole wheat flour, 1¼ cups unbleached all-purpose flour, ½ cup butter or shortening, and 4 tablespoons water. Proceed as above and bake according to the individual recipe directions.

Processor Single Pie Crust

PREPARATION TIME: 10 MINUTES
BAKING TIME: 15 MINUTES
YIELD: 1 SINGLE 9″ OR
    10″ PIE CRUST

1¼ cups unbleached all-
    purpose flour
¼ teaspoon salt
½ cup frozen butter
4 tablespoons ice water

Mix the flour and salt in a food processor bowl with the steel blade. Cut the butter into tablespoons and sprinkle over flour. Process with a pulsing on-and-off action until the texture resembles peas and cornmeal. Turn on the processor and add the water through the feed tube. As soon as the water is added, turn off the machine. It is not necessary for the dough to come together in a ball. Wrap the dough in a piece of plastic film and refrigerate for at least 1 hour, or until you are ready to use the pastry.

Roll the chilled dough out on a lightly floured board. Fit into a 9″ or 10″ pie pan and trim and crimp the edges. Fill the pie shell and bake according to the specific recipe directions.

To bake the crust unfilled, prick the dough with a fork, covering the surface of the pie shell with tiny holes that will allow steam to escape. Bake in a 450° oven for 10–15 minutes or until browned.

Variation

Processor Double Pie Crust. Use 2 cups unbleached all-purpose flour, ½ teaspoon salt, ¾ cup frozen butter, and 6 tablespoons ice water. Proceed as above and bake according to the individual recipe instructions.

Oil Single Pie Crust

PREPARATION TIME: 10 MINUTES
BAKING TIME: 10–15 MINUTES
YIELD: 1 SINGLE 9 " OR
   10" BOTTOM CRUST

1⅓ cups unbleached all-
   purpose flour
½ teaspoon salt
⅓ cup vegetable oil
2–3 tablespoons water

Oil crusts are not as flaky as butter or shortening crusts, but some people prefer them because they are lower in saturated fats.

In a medium-size mixing bowl, combine the flour and salt. Add the oil and water and stir until the dough comes together in a ball. Turn the ball out onto a lightly floured board. Flatten the ball, and roll it out to form a 12" circle. Lift the dough by loosely rolling it onto your rolling pin and fit the crust into a pie pan. Cut and crimp the edges. Fill the pie shell and bake according to specific recipe directions.

To bake unfilled, prick the dough with a fork, covering the surface of the pie shell with tiny holes that will allow steam to escape. Bake in a 450° F oven for 10–15 minutes or until browned.

Variation

Oil Double Pie Crust. Use 2 cups unbleached all-purpose flour, 1 teaspoon salt, ½ cup vegetable oil, and 2–3 tablespoons water. Proceed as above, and bake according to specific recipe instructions.

Basic Tart Crust

PREPARATION TIME: 10 MINUTES
BAKING TIME: ACCORDING TO
RECIPE DIRECTIONS
YIELD: 1 BOTTOM CRUST FOR
9″ TART

2 cups unbleached all-
purpose flour
½ cup butter
½ cup sugar
1 egg, beaten
2 tablespoons cold water

Place the flour in a bowl and cut in the butter until it resembles a mixture of peas. Add the sugar and stir well. Add the egg and water and mix until the dough comes together in a ball. Wrap the dough in plastic film wrap and chill at least 1 hour or until you are ready to use it.

On a lightly floured surface, slightly flatten the dough ball. Roll out the dough, working from the center to the edges until you have made a 10–11″ circle. Fold the dough in half and lift it onto a 9″ springform pan or tart pan. Unfold the dough and carefully fit it in the pan. If you prefer, you can press the dough into place with your fingers and the heel of your hand instead of rolling. Fold over the edge to make a 1½″ lip. Fill with the desired filling and bake according to the specific recipe directions.

Sweet Crust Variations for Pies and Tarts

Chocolate Crust. Substitute ½ cup cocoa in place of ½ cup flour for a single crust. Substitute ¾ cup cocoa in place of ¾ cup flour in a double crust recipe.

Nut Crust. Add ½ cup finely ground nuts with 1 tablespoon confectioners' sugar to a single crust recipe or ¾ cup finely ground nuts and 2 tablespoons confectioners' sugar to a double crust recipe.

Spice Crust. Add 1½ teaspoons of either cinnamon, cloves, mace, nutmeg, ginger, allspice, or a combination of spices to your crust recipe.

Coconut Crust. Add ½ cup shredded toasted coconut to the flour and shortening mixture in a single crust recipe. Add ¾ cup shredded coconut to a double crust recipe.

Orange-Flavored Crust. Use orange juice in place of water in making the crust. Add 1 tablespoon grated orange peel, if desired.

Lemon-Flavored Crust. Replace 2 tablespoons water with 2 tablespoons lemon juice. Add 2 tablespoons sugar and 1 tablespoon grated lemon rind to the crust.

Sesame Seed Crust. Add ¼ cup sesame seeds to the flour in a single crust recipe. Add ½ cup sesame seeds to a double crust recipe.

Almond Brown Sugar Tart Crust

PREPARATION TIME: 15 MINUTES
BAKING TIME: ACCORDING TO
   INDIVIDUAL RECIPE
   DIRECTIONS
YIELD: 1 DOUBLE CRUST FOR A
   9″ SPRINGFORM PAN

1¾ **cup unbleached all-
    purpose flour**
¼ **cup brown sugar**
¼ **cup ground almonds**
pinch salt
½ **cup butter**
1 **egg, slightly beaten**
1 **teaspoon vanilla extract**
½ **teaspoon almond extract**

In a medium-size mixing bowl, mix together the flour, sugar, ground almonds, and salt. Cut in the butter until the texture resembles coarse sand. Add the egg and vanilla and almond extracts. Stir until the dough comes together. Divide the dough into 2 round balls. Refrigerate for a least an hour or until you are ready to use the pastry.

On a lightly floured board, roll out half of the dough to form an 11″ circle. Fit the crust into a 9″ springform pan leaving a 1½″ rim. Trim the dough if necessary and save the scraps to make decorations on the top crust, if desired. Fill the crust with a fruit filling according to the recipe directions. Roll out the top crust and cover the filling. Decorate if desired.

If you are using only half the dough for a single crusted tart, roll out the remaining half and freeze.

Bake the tart according to specific recipe directions.

Bluebarb Pie

PREPARATION TIME: 30 MINUTES
BAKING TIME: 40 MINUTES
YIELD: 10" PIE

1 **double pie crust
(pages 80–86)**
3 **cups ½" rhubarb pieces**
2 **cups blueberries**
¼ **cup unbleached all-
purpose flour**
1 **cup sugar**
1 **tablespoon butter**
1 **egg, beaten**

You have heard of rhubarb pie and blueberry pie. With this combination, you have the sweetness of the blueberries matched to the body of the rhubarb.

Preheat the oven to 400° F.

Roll out the bottom crust and fit it into a 10" pie pan.

Mix together the fruit, flour, and sugar. Pour this mixture into the crust and dot with butter.

Roll out the top crust and place it over the fruit. Crimp the edges. Cut a few steam vents with a knife or fork. Brush the crust with the beaten egg and bake the pie for 20 minutes at 400° F. Turn the oven down to 350° F. and continue baking the pie for 20 minutes more. Remove the pie from the oven and allow the pie to cool for 30 minutes before cutting to allow the juice to set.

Variations

Rhubarb Pie. Use 5 cups cut rhubarb pieces and 1¾ cups sugar. Eliminate the blueberries.

Strawberry Rhubarb Pie. Substitute 2 cups sliced strawberries in place of the blueberries.

Spiced Rhubarb Peach Pie. Substitute 2 cups peeled and diced peaches in place of the blueberries. Substitute brown sugar for the white sugar and add 1 teaspoon cinnamon.

Apple Rhubarb Pie. Replace the blueberries with 2 cups peeled and sliced apples. Add ½ teaspoon cinnamon, ½ teaspoon cloves, and 1 teaspoon grated lemon rind.

Creamy Rhubarb Pie. Eliminate the blueberries. Increase the rhubarb to 5 cups and increase the sugar to 1¾ cups. Blend into the fruit mixture 3 egg yolks and ¼ cup sour cream.

Concord Grape Streusel Pie

PREPARATION TIME: 30 MINUTES
BAKING TIME: 40 MINUTES
YIELD: 9" PIE

Pie:

1 single pie crust
   (pages 79–86)
4 cups Concord grapes
¾ cup honey
¼ cup flour
3 tablespoons quick-cooking
   tapioca

Topping:

3 tablespoons butter, melted
½ cup granola
3 tablespoons honey

Preheat the oven to 425° F.

Roll out a single pie crust and fit it into a 9" pie pan.

Wash the grapes and remove the skins by pinching each grape and popping out the grape. (This is not as much work as it sounds!) Save the skins. Bring the pulp to a boil in a small saucepan and cook for 5 minutes, or until the pulp is soft. Press the pulp through a fine sieve, strainer, or food mill to remove the seeds. Combine the grape skins, grape pulp, flour, ¾ cup honey, and tapioca in a medium-size mixing bowl. Pour this mixture into the pie crust.

To make the topping, mix together the melted butter, granola, and 3 tablespoons honey. Sprinkle the topping evenly on top of the pie. Bake the pie for 40 minutes. Cool the pie before serving. It's excellent when served with vanilla ice cream.

Pumpkin Orange Chiffon Pie

PREPARATION TIME: 30 MINUTES
CHILLING TIME: 3 HOURS
YIELD: 10" PIE

1 10" baked pie crust
  (pages 79–86)
2 cups pumpkin puree
  (page 5)
1¼ cups brown sugar
½ teaspoon salt
½ teaspoon nutmeg
½ teaspoon cloves
½ teaspoon cinnamon
1 teaspoon ginger
⅓ cup orange juice
1 cup milk
1 cup sour cream
3 eggs, separated
2 tablespoons melted butter
2 tablespoons gelatin
¼ cup cold water
½ cup honey or sugar

Prepare the pie crust according to the recipe directions.

In the top of a double boiler, mix together the pumpkin, brown sugar, salt, spices, orange juice, milk, sour cream, egg yolks, and butter. Cook, stirring frequently, until the mixture thickens slightly, about 10 minutes.

In the meantime, sprinkle the gelatin over the cold water and set aside.

When the pumpkin mixture has thickened, remove it from the heat and stir in the gelatin. Blend well to be sure the gelatin is melted, and pour this mixture into the baked pie shell. Chill until set, about 2–3 hours.

When the pumpkin has set, beat the egg whites until frothy and soft peaks appear. Slowly add the honey or white sugar, and continue beating until the egg whites stand in firm peaks. Spread the meringue over the pie. Place the pie under a broiler for 3 minutes or until the meringue is golden.

Pumpkin Pie

PREPARATION TIME: 30 MINUTES
BAKING TIME: 45 MINUTES
YIELD: 10″ PIE

1 **single pie crust
(pages 79–86)**
2 **cups pumpkin puree
(page 5)**
3 **eggs**
1 **cup evaporated milk or
light cream**
¾ **cup honey or brown
sugar**
1 **teaspoon vanilla extract**
1 **teaspoon cinnamon**
½ **teaspoon ginger**
¼ **teaspoon cloves**
¼ **teaspoon allspice**

Preheat the oven to 350° F.
Roll out the pie crust and fit it into a 10″ pie pan.
Mix together the ingredients and pour the filling into the pie crust. Bake for 45 minutes. Cool before serving.

Variations

Mincemeat Pumpkin Pie. Spread 1½ cups Green Tomato Mincemeat (page 147) or Pear Mincemeat (page 148) on the bottom of the pie crust before you add the pumpkin filling.

Apple Butter Pumpkin Pie. Mix 1 cup Apple Butter (page 149) into the pumpkin puree. Decrease the honey to ¼ cup. Spread ½ cup apple butter on the bottom of the pie crust before you pour the pumpkin and apple filling in.

Pumpkin Pie With Pecan Caramel Topping. Mix together 3 tablespoons butter with ⅔ cup brown sugar. Sprinkle this mixture on top of the pie after it has baked and broil the topping for 2 minutes. Do not broil it longer or it will become syrupy.

Coconut Bourbon Pumpkin Pie. Add ¾ cup shredded coconut and ¼ cup bourbon to the pumpkin mixture and bake as directed. Cool the pie completely before serving.

Winter Squash Pie. Any of these pie variations can be made with 2 cups pureed winter squash (page 5) in place of the pumpkin.

Parsnip Pie. Replace the pumpkin in any of these pie variations with 2 cups pureed parsnips (page 5).

Carrot Pie. Replace the pumpkin in any of these pie variations with 2 cups pureed carrots (page 4).

Southern White Bean Pie

PREPARATION TIME: 30 MINUTES
BAKING TIME: 1 HOUR
YIELD: 10″ PIE

This pie tastes very similar to a pumpkin or squash pie.

1 **single pie crust
(pages 79–86)**

2 **cups white or navy beans
(⅔ pound uncooked)**

1½ **cups heavy cream or
evaporated milk**

½ **cup molasses**

½ **cup brown sugar**

2 **eggs**

1½ **teaspoons cinnamon**

½ **teaspoon ginger**

½ **teaspoon allspice**

½ **teaspoon mace**

12 **pecan halves
for garnishing**

Preheat the oven to 400° F.

Roll out the pie crust and carefully fit it into a 10″ pie pan.

It's best if the beans are cooked until they are very soft and will easily become smooth when pureed. Combine all the ingredients in a food processor, blender, or mixing bowl. Process until smooth.

Pour the filling into the prepared pie pan. Place the pecans around the top for decoration and bake for 1 hour, or until a knife inserted into the center comes out clean. Serve with sweetened whipped cream or ice cream.

Green Tomato Mincemeat Custard Pie

PREPARATION TIME: 15 MINUTES
BAKING TIME: 45 MINUTES
YIELD: 9″ PIE

1 single pie crust
  (pages 79–86)
1½ cups Green Tomato
  Mincemeat (page 147)
⅔ cup sugar or honey
1½ cups milk
1 teaspoon vanilla extract
3 eggs, beaten
½ cup almond slivers
1¼ teaspoons nutmeg

If you are short on time, consider making a custard dish without the pie crust. Just bake the custard in a greased 1-quart casserole or pie pan until the custard tests done, about 30–45 minutes.

Preheat the oven to 400° F.

Roll out the pie crust and fit it into a 9″ pie pan. Spread the mincemeat over the bottom of the crust.

Mix together the remaining ingredients, except the almonds and the nutmeg, to make a custard. Pour the custard over the mincemeat. Sprinkle the almonds and nutmeg on top. Bake the pie for 5 minutes at 400° F. Then reduce the heat to 350° F. and bake for 40 minutes or until the custard tests done. Serve this pie warm or cold.

Variations

Pear Mincemeat Custard Pie. Use 1½ cups Pear Mincemeat (page 148) in place of the Green Tomato Mincemeat.

Apple Butter Custard Pie. Use 1 cup Apple Butter (page 149) in place of the mincemeat and proceed with the recipe.

Rhubarb Custard Pie. Use 1½ cups Stewed Rhubarb (page 26) in place of the mincemeat. Drain the rhubarb to remove as much juice as possible. Then combine the juice with 2 teaspoons cornstarch and cook until the juice thickens. Serve the juice as a sauce to pour over the pie when it is served.

The Amazing No-Coconut Summer Squash Pie

PREPARATION TIME: 20 MINUTES
BAKING TIME: 55 MINUTES
YIELD: 10" PIE

I have almost stopped making real coconut pie because this pie is so good.

1 **single pie crust**
 (pages 79–86)
1½ **cups milk, half and half,**
 or cream
1½ **teaspoons unbleached**
 all-purpose flour
¾ **cup evaporated milk**
1 **cup sugar or honey**
3 **eggs, beaten**
½ **teaspoon salt**
¼ **teaspoon coconut extract**
¼ **teaspoon almond extract**
½ **teaspoon vanilla extract**
2 **cups summer squash**
 peeled, seeds removed, and
 grated
¼ **teaspoon nutmeg**

Preheat the oven to 400° F.

Roll out the pie crust and fit into a 10" pie pan.

In a small bowl, make a paste with 2 tablespoons of the milk and the flour.

In a large bowl, combine the evaporated milk, the remaining milk, half and half, or cream, the sweetener, eggs, salt, and extracts. Then mix the milk and flour paste into the custard mixture. Stir until smooth. Pour the custard into the pie crust. Sprinkle the summer squash evenly on top. Sprinkle with nutmeg.

Bake the pie for 15 minutes at 400° F. Turn the oven down to 325° F. and bake for 40 minutes more.

When the pie tests done, remove it from the oven and allow to cool to room temperature. Then chill well in the refrigerator. Serve with whipped cream, if desired.

Carrot Custard Pie

PREPARATION TIME: 20 MINUTES
BAKING TIME: 50 MINUTES
YIELD: 9" PIE

1 single pie crust
(pages 79–86)
4 eggs, slightly beaten
¼ teaspoon salt
½ cup maple syrup
3 cups milk, scalded
½ teaspoon lemon extract
1 teaspoon grated lemon rind
2 cups grated carrots
¼ teaspoon mace
¼ teaspoon allspice

Preheat the oven to 450° F.

Roll out the pastry dough and fit it into a 9" pie pan.

Mix together the eggs, salt, maple syrup, milk, lemon extract, lemon rind, and carrots. Pour the custard into the pie pan and sprinkle with the mace and allspice. Bake for 10 minutes at 450° F. Turn the oven down to 325° F. and bake for 40 minutes, or until the custard test done. Serve the pie warm or cold.

Variation

Parsnip Custard Pie. Substitute 2 cups of grated raw parsnips for the carrots. Add ¼ cup honey in addition to the maple syrup.

Shoo-Fly Sweet Potato Pie

PREPARATION TIME: 20 MINUTES
BAKING TIME: 50 MINUTES
YIELD: 10" PIE

1 **single pie crust**
  (pages 79–86)
4 **eggs**
1 **cup sugar**
1½ **cups dark corn syrup**
3 **tablespoons melted butter**
1 **teaspoon vanilla extract**
dash salt
1½ **cups pecan halves**
1 **cup grated raw sweet**
  potatoes

Preheat the oven to 350° F.

Roll out the pie crust and fit it into a 10" pie pan.

Mix together the eggs, sugar, corn syrup, butter, vanilla, and salt until blended.

Spread the nuts in the bottom of the pie crust and sprinkle on the sweet potatoes. Pour the egg mixture on top. Place the pie in the oven and lower the heat to 325° F. Bake the pie for 50 minutes. Cool before serving.

Variation

Shoo-Fly Carrot Pie. Substitute 2 cups grated raw carrots for the sweet potatoes.

Minted Peach Pie

PREPARATION TIME: 30 MINUTES
BAKING TIME: 45 MINUTES
YIELD: 10″ PIE

1 **double pie crust
(pages 80–86)**
4 **cups sliced, peeled peaches**
2½ **tablespoons quick-
cooking tapioca**
1½ **tablespoons cornstarch**
3 **tablespoons brown sugar**
3 **tablespoons sugar**
¼ **teaspoon cinnamon**
1 **teaspoon minced fresh mint
leaves**
2 **teaspoons lemon juice**

Preheat the oven to 425° F.

Roll out the bottom crust and carefully fit it into a 10″ pie pan.

Take 1 cup of the peach slices and puree in the blender. Combine the puree, tapioca, cornstarch, brown sugar, white sugar, and cinnamon in a small saucepan. Cook over medium heat until the mixture thickens.

Toss the remaining peach pieces with the mint and lemon juice. Mix in the peach puree mixture. Pour the filling into the pie pan and cover with the top crust. Crimp the edges and cut a few steam vents. Bake at 425° F. for 10 minutes. Reduce the heat to 350° F. and bake for 45 minutes.

Variations

Peach and Ginger Pie. Omit the mint and mix in 2 teaspoons ginger instead.

Peach and Strawberry Pie. Use 2 cups peach slices and 2 cups strawberries cut in quarters, instead of 4 cups peaches. Omit the mint.

Peach and Blueberry Pie. Use 2 cups peaches and 2 cups blueberries, instead of 4 cups peaches. Omit the mint.

Creamy Custard Strawberry Flan

PREPARATION TIME: 30 MINUTES
BAKING TIME: 20 MINUTES
YIELD: 12 SERVINGS

1 **single tart crust**
   (pages 85–87)
½ **cup cornstarch**
2 **cups milk**
2 **eggs, separated**
¼ **cup sugar or honey**
2 **cups strawberries**
½ **cup whipping cream**
   (optional)

Preheat the oven to 375° F.

Roll out the dough and fit it into a 9″ springform pan, leaving a 1½″ edge all around it. Prick the base with a fork in several places.

Bake the pastry for 20 minutes, then cool.

While the pastry bakes, prepare the filling. Blend the cornstarch and ¼ cup milk until smooth.

Separate the eggs. Beat the egg whites until soft peaks appear.

Scald the remaining milk, and add the cornstarch mixture and the sweetener. Return the pan to the stove and cook the milk mixture until it thickens, stirring continuously to prevent burning. Add the egg yolks and stir well. Remove the custard from the heat and continue stirring to allow the steam to escape.

Set aside 12 whole strawberries. Slice the rest.

When the custard has cooled down a little, fold the egg whites into it gently. Pour half of the custard mixture into the bottom of the pastry and place the sliced strawberries evenly over the top. Spread the remaining custard over the fruit and chill.

Just before serving, whip the cream and pipe onto the flan in 12 large stars or roses. Place a strawberry in each star.

Variations

Creamy Custard Raspberry Flan. Substitute 2 cups raspberries for the strawberries. Reserve 12 berries to decorate the top.

Creamy Custard Blackberry Flan. Substitute 2 cups blackberries for the strawberries. Reserve 12 berries to decorate the top.

Creamy Custard Peach Flan. Substitute 2 cups sliced, peeled peaches for the strawberries. Drop the peach slices along with 2 tablespoons lemon juice in water to cover to prevent browning. Reserve 12 slices to decorate the top.

Creamy Custard Pear Flan. Substitute 2 cups sliced, peeled pears for the strawberries. Drop the pear slices along with 2 tablespoons lemon juice in water to cover to prevent browning. Reserve 12 slices to decorate the top.

Creamy Custard Plum Flan. Substitute 2 cups quartered plums for the strawberries. Reserve 12 pieces to decorate the top.

Blueberry Almond Flan

PREPARATION TIME: 30 MINUTES
BAKING TIME: 40 MINUTES
YIELD: 8–12 SERVINGS

3 eggs, separated
½ cup sugar
1 cup ground almonds
1 teaspoon cinnamon
2 cups blueberries
1 single tart crust
   (pages 85–87)

The rich filling for this flan has ground nuts instead of flour to hold it together. It is deliciously different.

Beat the egg yolks with half of the sugar until it is thick and light yellow. In a separate bowl, beat the egg whites until frothy. Beat in the remaining sugar, 1 tablespoon at a time, until the egg whites are stiff.

Mix the ground nuts and cinnamon into the egg yolk mixture and fold in the egg whites. Mix the blueberries in gently.

Preheat the oven to 400° F.

Roll out the pastry on a floured board and carefully fit it into a 9″ springform pan, covering the bottom of the pan and making a rim 1½″ up the side of the pan. Prick the base with a fork in several places. Spoon the filling into the pastry shell and spread it evenly. Bake for 40 minutes.

Let the pastry cool slightly before removing the sides of the pan. Cool completely before serving.

Pear Almond Tart

PREPARATION TIME: 30 MINUTES
BAKING TIME: 1¼ HOURS
YIELD: 9″ TART

1 **single tart crust
(pages 85–87)**
1 **cup blanched almonds**
6 **tablespoons butter at room
temperature**
⅓ **cup sugar**
3 **pears, peeled**
3 **cups cold water**
1 **tablespoon lemon juice**
1 **tablespoon apricot
preserves**
1 **teaspoon water**

Preheat the oven to 350° F.

Roll out the tart crust or press into a 9″ tart pan or springform pan.

In a food processor or with a hand grinder, grind the almonds finely. If you use the processor, add 2 tablespoons of the sugar to the nuts to prevent them from sticking together. Add the butter and the remaining sugar to the nuts, and cream them together until the mixture is light and fluffy. Spread the almond mixture evenly over the bottom of the crust.

As you peel the pears, drop them in the water and lemon juice to prevent browning. Slice each pear in half and remove the core. Then slice each pear into ¼″ slices, cutting from side to side (not from stem end to the bottom). Keep the slices together. Place your hand on top of the sliced pear and press it forward to fan out the slices. Carefully pick up the slices with a spatula and place them on the tart with the neck, or top, of the pear facing the center of the tart. Continue cutting the pears and setting them in place.

In a small saucepan, melt the apricot jam with the water and brush the top of the tart all over with this mixture.

Bake for 1¼ hours. Serve cool.

Variation

Apple Almond Tart. Use peeled, sliced apples in place of the pears, being sure to fan them out as instructed for the pears. Sprinkle the apples with 1 tablespoon sugar and ½ teaspoon cinnamon before brushing on the glaze.

Blackberry Tart With Meringue Top

PREPARATION TIME: 30 MINUTES
BAKING TIME: 35 MINUTES
YIELD: 9" TART

Tart:

1 single tart crust
  (pages 85–87)
3 cups blackberries
¼ cup honey
1 tablespoon water
3 teaspoons cornstarch

Meringue:

3 egg whites
¼ cup honey

Preheat the oven to 400° F.

Roll out the crust and fit it gently into a 9" springform pan, making a 1" rim all around. Prick the crust bottom. Bake for 20 minutes, then cool.

In a small saucepan, combine the blackberries and honey, and simmer on medium heat. Mix the cornstarch and water to form a paste, and add this to the fruit. Cook the fruit until the cornstarch mixture turns clear (not white) and the mixture has thickened. Remove the fruit from the heat, and cool slightly.

In a clean, dry mixing bowl, beat the egg whites until they are frothy. As you continue to beat the egg whites, drizzle in the ¼ cup honey in a slow thin thread, until the egg whites stand in peaks.

Spread the blackberry mixture onto the crust. Using a piping bag, pipe the beaten egg whites in a crisscross pattern on the top. Bake for 15 minutes to brown the meringue slightly. Cool before serving.

Variations

Raspberry Tart With Meringue Top. Substitute 3 cups raspberries for the blackberries.

Strawberry Tart With Meringue Top. Substitute 3 cups strawberries for the blackberries.

Peach Tart With Meringue Top. Substitute 3 cups peeled and sliced peaches for the blackberries.

Plum Tart With Meringue Top. Substitute 3 cups quartered plums for the blackberries.

Cream Cheese Strawberry Tart

PREPARATION TIME: 30 MINUTES
COOLING TIME: 2 HOURS
YIELD: 9″ TART

8 ounces cream cheese at
    room temperature
2-4 tablespoons honey or
    sugar
¼ cup plain yogurt
1 tablespoon grated lemon
    rind
1 tablespoon lemon juice
¼ teaspoon almond extract
¼ cup ground almonds
1 single prebaked and cooled
    9″ tart pastry (pages 85–87)
2-3 cups whole strawberries
2 tablespoons apricot jam
1 teaspoon water

Cream together the cream cheese, sweetener, yogurt, lemon rind, lemon juice, almond extract, and almonds. Spread this mixture in the cooled tart shell. Trim the strawberries so they will sit flat. Arrange the berries in concentric circles over the cream cheese layer.

In a small saucepan, heat the jam with the water and brush it over the fruit. Chill the tart until the cream cheese sets (about 2 hours).

Variations

Cream Cheese Plum Tart. Substitute 2–3 cups quartered plums for the strawberries. Brush with a glaze made of 2 tablespoons red raspberry jam and 1 teaspoon water.

Cream Cheese Cantaloupe Tart. Substitute 1 melon cut in very thin 1″ wedges for the strawberries. Overlap the melon pieces to completely cover the cream cheese.

Cream Cheese Honeydew Tart. Substitute 1 honeydew melon cut in very thin 1″ wedges for the strawberries. Overlap the melon pieces to completely cover the cream cheese.

Cream Cheese Pear Tart. Substitute 2–3 cups peeled, thinly sliced pears for the strawberries. Place the pears in water to cover with 1 tablespoon lemon juice to prevent them from browning before arranging on top of the tart. Brush with a glaze made of 2 tablespoons red raspberry jam and 1 teaspoon water.

Cream Cheese Blueberry Tart. Substitute 2–3 cups blueberries for the strawberries. Brush with a glaze made with 2 tablespoons red raspberry jam and 1 teaspoon water.

Cream Cheese Kiwi Fruit Tart. Substitute 3–4 peeled, thinly sliced kiwi fruits for the strawberries.

Cream Cheese Blackberry Tart. Substitute 2–3 cups blackberries for the strawberries. Brush with a glaze made with 2 tablespoons red raspberry jam and 1 teaspoon water.

Cream Cheese Peach Tart. Substitute 2–3 cups peeled and sliced peaches for the strawberries. Place the peaches in water to cover with 1 tablespoon lemon juice to prevent browning before arranging on top of the tart. Use either 2 tablespoons apricot jam and 1 teaspoon water or 2 tablespoons red raspberry jam and 1 teaspoon water for the glaze.

French Apple Tart

PREPARATION TIME: 30 MINUTES
BAKING TIME: 1 HOUR
YIELD: 9″ TART

2 pounds apples
1 lemon, juice and rind
1 single tart crust
   (pages 85–87)
3 eggs
½ cup sugar or honey
½ cup heavy cream
1 teaspoon vanilla extract

Peel and quarter the apples and remove the cores. Slice each quarter most of the way through, making several thin slices that are still connected at the bottom. Place the apples in water to cover. Add the lemon juice to prevent apples from browning and set aside.

Preheat the oven to 400° F.

Roll the dough out on a lightly floured board until it is about 12″ in diameter. Fit it into a 9″ springform pan, leaving edges of 1½″. Prick the bottom in several places with a fork. Arrange the apple quarters on top. Bake for 20 minutes.

While the tart bakes, beat together eggs and sweetener until the mixture is light yellow in color. Add the cream, vanilla, and grated lemon rind. Pour the custard mixture into the tart and bake for 30 minutes. Remove from the oven and allow the tart to cool before serving.

Rhubarb Crisscross Tart

PREPARATION TIME: 30 MINUTES
BAKING TIME: 40 MINUTES
YIELD: 10 SERVINGS

**1 single tart crust
(pages 85–87)**
2 pounds rhubarb
½ cup honey
3 egg whites

Preheat the oven to 400° F.

On a floured surface, roll out the tart crust dough to make a rectangle that is slightly larger than a cookie sheet. Lift the dough onto the cookie sheet and trim to fit in the pan with a slight overlap. Pinch the overlap to form a 1″ rim. Prick the dough with a fork in several places.

Cut the rhubarb into 3″ pieces. Place the rhubarb on the dough in even rows. Drizzle ¼ cup honey over the rhubarb. Bake the tart for 30 minutes.

While the tart bakes, beat the egg whites until they are almost stiff. Drizzle in the remaining honey, a little at a time, as you continue whipping the egg whites to make a thick meringue that stands in stiff peaks. Place the meringue in a pastry bag fitted with a star tip. When the tart is baked, pipe out the meringue in a diagonal crisscross pattern. Or spread the meringue over the top using a spatula. Brown the topping for 10 minutes in the oven. Serve the tart warm.

Cheesecakes

Very little can go wrong with a cheesecake. If your ingredients are warmed to room temperature before mixing, you are guaranteed that the mixture will whip into a smooth creamy dessert.

The one problem people seem to have with cheesecakes is that the top often cracks. At least 95 percent of the time you can avoid this by leaving the cheesecake in the oven with the door open to cool slowly to room temperature. Then refrigerate.

If you are putting a topping on the cheesecake, it is best to add it onto a chilled cake. Just before serving, remove the sides of the springform pan.

Along with recipes for cheesecakes that call for specific fruits and vegetables, we have included recipes for basic cheesecakes (made with cream cheese, cottage cheese and yogurt, and tofu) and several different pie crust variations. You can use these cheesecakes with several different fruit toppings. Arrange fresh berries, or sliced peaches, apples, plums, pears, cherries, or kiwi fruit on a plain cheesecake. Or serve with a Blueberry Orange Sauce (page 143) or Sour Cherry Sauce (page 143) poured over the cheesecake just before serving.

Cookie Crusts for Cheesecakes

PREPARATION TIME: 10 MINUTES
YIELD: 9″ CHEESECAKE CRUST
 (OR PIE CRUST)

These crusts are very easy to make and are good with ice cream pies as well as cheesecakes.

Any dry, homemade cookie or cake crumbs will work fine with these recipes. Start with completely dry cookies. If your cookies still have moisture in them, bake them in the oven at 200° F. for 15 minutes. Then fit your food processor with a steel blade and process the cookies until you have fine crumbs. It is a good idea to break up the cookies with your hands before processing. If you don't have a food processor, place the cookies in a plastic bag, close the bag with a knot or twist tie. Then roll over the cookies with a rolling pin until they are a consistent fine powder.

Graham Cracker Crust. Crush ⅓ package of graham crackers (11 crackers). Mix in ¼ cup melted butter. Press the crust 1″ up the sides of a 9″ springform pan and over the bottom of the pan. Pour in the cheesecake batter and bake according to the cheesecake recipe directions.

Gingersnap Cookie Crust. Crush 30 gingersnap cookies to make 2 cups of crumbs. Combine with ¼ cup melted butter and press into a 9″ springform pan, as above.

Chocolate Cookie Crust. Crush an 8-ounce package of Famous brand Chocolate Wafers. Combine ¼ cup melted butter and press into a 9″ springform pan, as above.

Granola Crust. Process 2 cups of granola in a food processor or blender until the oats are broken up and finely ground. Add ½ teaspoon cinnamon and mix in ¼ cup melted butter. Press the crust into a 9″ springform pan, as above.

Zwieback Crust. Crush 12 zwieback crackers to make 2 cups of crumbs. Add ½ teaspoon cinnamon and 2 tablespoons sugar (optional) and mix in ¼ cup melted butter. Press the crust into a 9″ springform pan, as above.

Oatmeal Pecan Cheesecake Crust

PREPARATION TIME: 10 MINUTES
YIELD: 9″ CHEESECAKE CRUST

1 cup quick cooking rolled
   oats
¾ cup pecans
½ teaspoon cinnamon
2 tablespoons brown sugar,
   firmly packed
¼ cup butter, melted

Combine the oatmeal, pecans, cinnamon, and brown sugar in a food processor or blender and process until the nuts and oats are chopped. Pour this mixture into a 9″ springform pan and add the melted butter. Mix well and press the crust 1″ up the sides of the pan and flat across the bottom of the pan. Pour in the cheesecake filling and bake according to the cheesecake recipe directions.

Basic Cheesecake

PREPARATION TIME: 20 MINUTES
BAKING TIME: 1 HOUR
YIELD: 12 SERVINGS

1 cheesecake crust
 (pages 108–109)
1 pound cream cheese at
 room temperature
4 eggs
1 cup sour cream
1 cup white sugar or ½ cup
 honey or 1 cup brown
 sugar, firmly packed
1 teaspoon vanilla extract

Preheat the oven to 350° F.

In a food processor or a mixing bowl, cream the cream cheese. Add the eggs, one at a time, and blend well after each addition. Add the sour cream, sweetener, and vanilla. Blend well, scraping down the sides of the bowl. Be sure there are no lumps in the cheese mixture; they will not blend in during baking. Pour the cheesecake into the crust and bake for 1 hour. Turn the oven off after 1 hour and leave the oven door open until the inside of the oven reaches room temperature. Chill the cheesecake before serving. Decorate the top with fruit or your favorite fruit topping and serve.

Variations

Apple Butter Cheesecake. After the batter has been poured into the crust, spoon in ¾ cup Apple Butter (page 149) in evenly distributed spoonfuls. The Apple Butter will sink to the bottom. Sprinkle the top of the cheesecake with ½ cup ground almonds and bake as directed above.

Pear Butter Cheesecake. After the batter has been poured into the crust, spoon in ¾ cup Pear Butter (page 149) in evenly distributed spoonfuls. The Pear Butter will sink to the bottom. Sprinkle the top of the cheesecake with ½ cup ground almonds and bake as directed above.

Apple Spice Cheesecake

PREPARATION TIME: 45 MINUTES
BAKING TIME: 1¼ HOURS
YIELD: 12 SERVINGS

Crust:

1 cup unbleached all-
  purpose flour
¼ cup sugar
¼ cup butter
½ cup ground almonds
1 egg

Apple Mixture:

4 apples, peeled and sliced
½ cup water
¼ cup sugar
1 teaspoon cinnamon

Cheesecake:

8 ounces cream cheese at
  room temperature
1 cup cottage cheese
1 cup sour cream
¾ cup brown sugar
4 eggs
½ teaspoon cinnamon
2 tablespoons butter, melted
1 tablespoon sugar

Preheat the oven to 350° F. Mix together the flour and sugar for the crust. Cut in the butter and add the ground almonds. Add the egg, and mix to form the dough. Press the dough into a 9″ springform pan, and bake for 15 minutes.

While the crust bakes, slice the apples. Simmer the apples in ½ cup of water for 5 minutes to soften them. Drain well and reserve half of the apple slices to garnish the cake. Mix the sugar and cinnamon with the remaining apples.

In a food processor or a mixer, combine the cream cheese, cottage cheese, sour cream, brown sugar, eggs, and cinnamon. Mix until completely smooth.

Spread the spiced apple mixture on top of the baked crust. Pour the cheese mixture on top. Push down any apple slices that rise up. Bake for 45 minutes.

Remove the cake from the oven and arrange the reserved apple slices neatly in rows to cover the top of the cake. Brush with the melted butter, and sprinkle with sugar. Return the cake to the oven for 15 minutes more. Then quickly broil the cake for 5 minutes to brown the apples on top. Cool the cake completely before serving.

Yogurt Cottage Cheesecake

PREPARATION TIME: 20 MINUTES
BAKING TIME: 1 HOUR
YIELD: 10 SERVINGS

**1 cheesecake crust
(pages 108–109)
2 cups cottage cheese
3 eggs
1 egg yolk
⅓ cup honey
½ cup yogurt
1½ teaspoons vanilla extract
¼ cup unbleached all-
purpose flour
grated rind from 1 lemon
1 tablespoon lemon juice**

Preheat the oven to 325° F.

Prepare the crust and press it into a 9″ springform pan.

Put the cottage cheese in a food processor and blend until smooth. Add the remaining ingredients and process until smooth. If you don't have a processor, use a blender and combine all the ingredients at once and blend until smooth.

Pour the filling into the crust and bake for 1 hour. Leave the cheesecake in the oven with the door open until the inside of the oven reaches room temperature. Chill the cheesecake. Just before serving, remove the sides of the pan. Serve with fruit or top with Carrot Apricot Topping (page 113).

Tofu Cheesecake

PREPARATION TIME: 20 MINUTES
BAKING TIME: 1 HOUR
YIELD: 12 SERVINGS

1 cheesecake crust
   (pages 108–109)
3 cups (1½ pounds)
   crumbled tofu
¼ cup fresh lemon juice
grated rind from 1 lemon
½ cup honey
½ cup butter, melted

Preheat the oven to 350° F.

In a food processor or blender, combine all the ingredients and blend until smooth. Pour the batter into a prepared cheesecake crust and bake for 1 hour. Chill well before serving. Decorate the top with your favorite fruit topping and serve.

Carrot Apricot Topping for Cheesecake

PREPARATION TIME: 30 MINUTES
YIELD: 1½ CUPS

4 ounces dried apricots
½ cup water or more
2 tablespoons honey
2 tablespoons butter
1 cup grated carrot
1 tablespoon orange juice
1 tablespoon Grand Marnier
   (optional)

Combine the apricots and water in a saucepan and simmer for 15 minutes. Add the honey, butter, and carrots to the apricots. Add more water if necessary to prevent the mixture from burning. Continue cooking for another 15 minutes. Remove from the heat and place in a blender or food processor. Add the orange juice and liqueur. Blend the mixture until smooth. It should be quite thick. Add more orange juice if necessary to make the mixture spreadable. Cool the topping.

Make your favorite cheesecake and cool. Spread the cooled topping on the cheesecake. Chill to set.

Carrot Cheesecake

PREPARATION TIME: 30 MINUTES
BAKING TIME: 1 HOUR
YIELD: 12 SERVINGS

1 graham cracker crust (page 108)
1 pound cream cheese at room temperature
1 cup sour cream
4 eggs
1 cup brown sugar or white sugar, or ¾ cup honey
1½ cups carrot puree (page 4)
1 teaspoon cinnamon
½ teaspoon ginger
dash nutmeg

Preheat the oven to 325° F.

Mix together the ingredients for the graham cracker crust. Press the mixture into a 9″ springform pan. Make a ½″ rim around the edge.

Cream together the cream cheese and the sour cream. Beat in the eggs, one at a time. Blend in the sweetener, the carrot puree, and the spices. Continue mixing until the mixture is completely smooth. Pour the cheesecake batter into the crumb crust. Place the cheesecake on the central rack of the oven and bake for 1 hour. Open the oven door and allow the cheesecake to cool to room temperature before refrigerating. Chill completely and cut into 12 slices to serve.

Variations

Pumpkin Cheesecake. Substitute 1½ cups pumpkin puree (page 5) for the carrot puree.

Winter Squash Cheesecake. Substitute 1½ cups winter squash puree (page 5) for the carrot puree.

White Cloud Cheesecake With Peaches

PREPARATION TIME: 25 MINUTES
BAKING TIME: 40 MINUTES
YIELD: 10 SERVINGS

1 **single tart crust
(pages 85–87)**
2 **cups cottage cheese**
2 **eggs, separated**
¾ **cup confectioners' sugar**
2 **tablespoons cornstarch**
1 **teaspoon grated lemon rind**
1 **teaspoon grated orange
rind**
1 **teaspoon vanilla extract**
1½ **cups peeled and sliced
peaches**
1 **tablespoon sugar**

Preheat the oven to 375° F.

Fit the tart crust into a 9" tart pan or springform pan, allowing 1½" of pastry to cover the sides of the pan. Prebake the crust for 15 minutes.

In a food processor or blender, mix the cottage cheese, egg yolks, ½ cup confectioners' sugar, cornstarch, lemon and orange rinds, and vanilla.

Beat the egg whites until stiff peaks form. Beat in the remaining ¼ cup confectioners' sugar. Fold the egg whites into the cheese mixture.

Lay the sliced peaches on the bottom of the tart and sprinkle with 1 tablespoon granulated sugar. Spoon the cheesecake mixture on top of the peaches. Bake for 40 minutes. Cool the cake before serving.

Variations

White Cloud Cheesecake With Plums. Substitute 1½ cups quartered plums in place of the peaches. Simmer the plums in 1 cup of water to soften, then drain well for 5 minutes before arranging on the bottom of the crust.

White Cloud Cheesecake With Blueberries. Substitute 1½ cups blueberries in place of the peaches.

White Cloud Cheesecake With Pears. Peel and slice 3–4 pears to make 1½ cups peeled, sliced pears and use in place of the peaches.

White Cloud Cheesecake With Raspberries. Substitute 1½ cups raspberries for the peaches.

Beetific Cheesecake

PREPARATION TIME: 20 MINUTES
BAKING TIME: 20 MINUTES
YIELD: 8–10 SERVINGS

1 **single tart crust**
   (pages 85–87)
3 **eggs, separated**
8 **ounces cream cheese at**
   room temperature
¼ **cup honey**
⅓ **cup pureed beets**
   (page 4)
grated rind from 1 lemon
½ **teaspoon almond extract**
½ **teaspoon vanilla extract**

This cheesecake has an unbelievable color and a lovely light texture. Serve it on Valentine's Day and to those who love pink.

Preheat the oven to 350° F. Roll out the crust and fit it into a 9″ springform pan. Bake the crust for 10 minutes.

While the crust bakes, beat the egg whites until stiff. Mix together the cream cheese, honey, egg yolks, and beet puree until smooth. Add the lemon rind and the almond and vanilla extracts. Fold the egg whites into the beet mixture. Pour the batter into the crust. Bake the cheesecake for 20 minutes. Chill well before serving.

Cobblers,
Crisps, and Strudels

There's nothing glamorous about a cobbler or a crisp, but that's why I like them. They embody the pioneer spirit of inventiveness, and indeed, many of these recipes go way back to the homesteaders who stocked their larders but once or twice a year. Those clever women learned to bake from the basics they had on hand. So you find cobblers and crisps made with flour, oatmeal, bread crumbs, or even stale bread. With the simple dough, they baked whatever fruit they had on hand: storage apples, or preserved peaches or pears. In the summer, of course, there was fresh fruit to choose from. These days, we can enjoy the same desserts, even pulling berries from the freezer to enjoy all winter long.

Strudels aren't American in origin, but that same make-do approach to desserts is apparent here. The strudel dough is fairly simple, and the fruit fillings can be made from whatever is on hand.

Corn Berry Cobbler

PREPARATION TIME: 20 MINUTES
BAKING TIME: 1 HOUR
YIELD: 6 SERVINGS

1 quart strawberry halves
¾ cup honey
1 cup cornmeal
1 teaspoon baking powder
½ teaspoon salt
4 tablespoons butter, melted
½ cup buttermilk or yogurt
1 tablespoon lemon juice

Preheat the oven to 350° F.

Butter a 2-quart baking dish and arrange the strawberries in it. Drizzle ¼ cup of the honey over the berries.

Mix together the cornmeal, baking powder, salt, 2 tablespoons of the butter, and the buttermilk or yogurt. Drop the batter by tablespoons onto the berries.

Mix together the remaining honey, butter, and the lemon juice. Pour this sauce on top of the batter and bake for 1 hour. Serve warm. It is delicious with ice cream.

Apple Brown Betty

PREPARATION TIME: 20 MINUTES
BAKING TIME: 45 MINUTES
YIELD: 6 SERVINGS

4 cups peeled, cored and sliced apples
1 cup wheat germ
½ cup whole wheat flour or unbleached all-purpose flour
1 teaspoon cinnamon
½ cup brown sugar or honey
4 tablespoons butter, melted
juice of 1 lemon

Many people use bread crumbs to make Apple Brown Betty, but I much prefer the rich nutty flavor of wheat germ, and it's so much better for you.

Preheat the oven to 350° F.

Place half of the apples in a greased, 1-quart baking dish and sprinkle with lemon juice.

Mix the remaining ingredients together. Sprinkle half of the mixture on top of the apples. Place the remaining apples in the pan and cover with the remaining topping. Bake for 45 minutes, or until the apples are soft and the topping is crunchy.

Variations

Peach Brown Betty. Substitute 4 cups peeled and sliced peaches for the apples.

Pear Brown Betty. Substitute 4 cups peeled and sliced pears for the apples.

Plum Brown Betty. Substitute 4 cups quartered plums for the apples.

Apple Crisp

PREPARATION TIME: 20 MINUTES
BAKING TIME: 45 MINUTES
YIELD: 8–10 SERVINGS

Filling:

5 large apples, peeled
  and sliced
1 teaspoon cinnamon
1 teaspoon nutmeg
1 tablespoon lemon juice
grated rind from 1 lemon

Topping:

¾ cup brown sugar
½ cup chopped walnuts
½ cup unbleached all-
  purpose flour
½ cup butter at room
  temperature
1 cup rolled oats
¼ teaspoon salt
½ teaspoon cinnamon

Preheat the oven to 350° F.

In a medium-size mixing bowl, mix together all the filling ingredients. Toss until the apples are coated. Butter a 2-quart baking dish and pour in the apples.

Mix together all the topping ingredients and sprinkle over the apples. Bake for 1 hour. Serve warm with ice cream.

Variations

Peach Crisp. Use 5 large peaches, peeled and sliced, in place of the apples.

Plum Crisp. Use 4 cups quartered plums in place of the apples.

Pear Crisp. Use 6 pears, peeled and sliced, in place of the apples.

Cherry Crisp. Mix 4 cups of sour cherries with ¼ cup sugar and use in place of the apples. Omit the lemon juice.

Apple Pandowdy

PREPARATION TIME: 30 MINUTES
BAKING TIME: 1 HOUR
YIELD: 6–8 SERVINGS

Pandowdies are a native New England dish made from fruit and sweetened either in part or completely with molasses. Pie dough is placed on top of the fruit and baked until golden brown. This hearty dessert is delicious served with cream poured over it.

4 cups peeled, cored, and
　sliced apples
¼ cup molasses
¼ cup honey or brown
　sugar
1 teaspoon cinnamon
¼ teaspoon allspice
1 tablespoon lemon juice
1 single pie crust
　(pages 79–86)
1 egg, beaten

Preheat the oven to 350° F.

Grease a 2-quart baking dish and place the apples in it. Mix in the molasses, honey or brown sugar, cinnamon, allspice, and lemon juice.

Prepare a single pie crust and roll it out to fit on top of the fruit. Crimp the edges and brush with beaten egg. Bake for 1 hour.

Variations

Peach Pandowdy. Substitute 4 cups peeled and sliced peaches for the apples.

Plum Pandowdy. Substitute 4 cups quartered plums for the apples.

Pear Pandowdy. Substitute 4 cups peeled and sliced pears for the apples.

Apple Cobbler

PREPARATION TIME: 30 MINUTES
BAKING TIME: 1⅓ HOURS
YIELD: 6 SERVINGS

4 cups peeled, cored, and
   sliced apples
1½ teaspoons cinnamon
juice from ½ lemon
1 cup sugar or honey
1 cup unbleached all-
   purpose flour
½ cup whole wheat flour
2 teaspoons baking powder
½ teaspoon salt
2 eggs
¾ cup milk
4 tablespoons melted butter
1 teaspoon vanilla extract
1 cup heavy cream (optional)

Cobblers can be made with fresh raw fruits or with canned or frozen fruits. Just about any fruit is delicious prepared in this way.

Preheat the oven to 350° F.

Place the apples in a greased 2-quart baking dish and mix in 1 teaspoon cinnamon and the lemon juice. Drizzle ½ cup sugar or honey on top. Bake for 20 minutes.

While the apples bake, sift together the flours, baking powder, salt, and remaining cinnamon. Mix together the eggs, milk, butter, vanilla, and remaining sweetener. Combine the dry ingredients and wet ingredients, and beat until smooth. Pour the batter over the fruit and bake uncovered for 1 hour or until the cake pulls away from the sides of the pan. Serve warm with heavy cream to pour over it.

Variations

Rhubarb Cobbler. Substitute 4 cups sliced rhubarb for the apples.

Berry Cobbler. Substitute 4 cups blackberries, raspberries, blueberries, or strawberries for the apples. Do not prebake the berries.

Pear Cobbler. Substitute 4 cups peeled and sliced pears for the apples. If you are using canned pears, do not prebake the fruit. Adjust the sweetener to taste if the pears are in a sugar syrup.

Peach Cobbler. Substitute 4 cups peeled and sliced peaches for the apples. If you are using canned peaches, do not prebake the fruit. Adjust the sweetener to taste if the peaches are preserved in a sugar syrup.

Apple Charlotte

PREPARATION TIME: 30 MINUTES
BAKING TIME: 45 MINUTES
YIELD: 8 SERVINGS

**8 tart apples, peeled and
  sliced**
¾ cup butter
¼ cup brown sugar
grated rind from 1 lemon
1 tablespoon lemon juice
½ teaspoon cloves
½ teaspoon allspice
¼ cup apricot jam
**10–12 slices whole wheat
  bread**

Preheat the oven to 400° F.

In a medium-size saucepan, melt ¼ cup of the butter and toss in the apples. Sauté them for 5 minutes, stirring gently. Add the brown sugar, lemon rind, lemon juice, spices, and apricot jam. Continue cooking over medium heat for 5 minutes.

Grease a 1½-quart baking dish. Melt the remaining butter. Trim the crusts off the bread. Cut the bread into pieces so they can completely line the baking dish. Sauté the bread in the melted butter until lightly toasted on one side. Line the baking dish with the bread, setting aside a few pieces for the top. Pour in the apple mixture and cover with the remaining bread slices. Bake for 45 minutes. Serve warm.

Baked Apple Dumplings

PREPARATION TIME: 30 MINUTES
BAKING TIME: 45 MINUTES
YIELD: 6 SERVINGS

6 apples, peeled and cored
dough for a single pie crust
 (pages 79–86)
½ cup brown sugar
¼ cup butter
¼ teaspoon salt
½ teaspoon cinnamon
½ teaspoon nutmeg
½ teaspoon grated lemon
 rind
½ cup chopped nuts
¼ cup raisins
1 beaten egg

Preheat the oven to 350° F.

Roll out the pastry to ⅛″ thick. Cut into squares large enough to wrap around the apples.

Combine the brown sugar, butter, salt, spices, lemon rind, nuts, and raisins. Stuff the apples with the brown sugar mixture. Wrap the dough around the apples and place the dumplings in an 8″ × 8″ baking dish, seam side down. Brush the dumplings with the beaten egg. Bake for 45 minutes.

Variation

Baked Pear Dumplings. Substitute 6 pears for the apples.

Apple Strudel

PREPARATION TIME: 30 MINUTES
BAKING TIME: 40 MINUTES
YIELD: 12–15 SERVINGS

The filo dough called for in this recipe can be purchased at most supermarkets in the deli section or at specialty food shops. The dough comes frozen and can be stored indefinitely.

Defrost filo dough completely before using it. Keep a damp towel over the dough that you are not working with to prevent it from drying out. Sometimes the sheets of dough stick together or tear. Just patch torn sheets together and use full, untorn sheets on top. Wrap unused dough in plastic film and refreeze for another time.

6 **cups peeled, sliced apples (4–6 apples)**
1 **cup bread crumbs**
2 **tablespoons lemon juice**
5 **tablespoons brown sugar or honey**
1 **teaspoon cinnamon**
¼ **teaspoon mace**
1 **cup butter, melted**
½ **cup raisins**
16–20 **sheets filo dough**

Preheat the oven to 400° F.

Plump the raisins by pouring boiling water over them and letting them soak for 5 minutes. Then drain the water.

Mix together the apples, bread crumbs, lemon juice, sweetener, spices, ½ cup melted butter, and the raisins.

On a dry work surface, lay down 2 sheets of filo dough on top of each other. Place 2 more sheets of filo dough beside the first sheets, with a 2" overlap, and brush the sheets with butter. Continue placing sheets of filo dough on top of the original piles, overlapping them in the same fashion. Brush butter on every other layer.

Place the apple mixture in the middle of the dough in a rectangular pile. Fold the ends of the dough over the apples, and roll the filo to completely seal in the apples. Place the strudel on a greased cookie sheet and brush with butter. Bake for 40 minutes or until the top is brown. Serve warm.

Austrian Plum Strudel

PREPARATION TIME: 1 HOUR
BAKING TIME: 40 MINUTES
YIELD: 12 SERVINGS

This is a tart strudel. If you like, increase the sugar or honey in the filling.

Crust:

1 tablespoon butter, melted
2 tablespoons warm water
1 egg
2 cups plus 1 tablespoon unbleached all-purpose flour

Filling:

2 pounds (about 35) prune plums (6 cups prepared fruit)
11 tablespoons butter
1 cup bread crumbs
5 tablespoons sugar or honey
½ cup chopped walnuts
¼ teaspoon cloves

To make the crust, combine 1 tablespoon melted butter with the water and egg in a medium-size mixing bowl. Sift the flour into the wet ingredients. Stir well until the dough forms a ball. Knead the dough briefly. Place the dough back in the bowl, cover, and set aside for 45–60 minutes.

While the dough rests, wash, pit, and quarter the plums. Melt the remaining butter and reserve 3 tablespoons of the butter. Mix the remaining butter with the bread crumbs, sugar, walnuts, cloves, and plums. Preheat the oven to 350° F.

On a lightly floured surface, roll the dough out as thin as possible without tearing it. If the dough tears, pinch it back together and continue rolling it out. Some cooks stretch the dough instead of rolling it. This is done by placing your hands under the dough, knuckle side up, and gently stretching the dough.

Spread the plum mixture over two-thirds of the dough. Brush the remaining third of the dough with butter. Roll up the strudel starting at the end with the fruit.

Place the rolled strudel on a greased cookie sheet and brush the top with melted butter. Bake for 40 minutes. Dust with confectioners' sugar before serving.

Serve the strudel warm.

Variation

Peach Strudel. Use 6 cups peeled and sliced peaches instead of the plums. Add 1 teaspoon cinnamon to the bread crumbs.

Blueberry Grunt

PREPARATION TIME: 20 MINUTES
COOKING TIME: 20 MINUTES
YIELD: 6–8 SERVINGS

1 cup whipping cream
2 cups unbleached all-
    purpose flour
½ teaspoon salt
4 teaspoons baking powder
½ teaspoon cream of tartar
⅓ cup milk
2 pints fresh blueberries
⅓ cup honey or sugar
½ cup water
1 tablespoon lemon juice
1 tablespoon butter

Whip the cream. Sift together the flour, salt, baking powder, and cream of tartar. Fold the dry ingredients and the milk in with the cream. Stir just enough to mix. Set the dough aside.

In a large flat-bottomed frying pan with a lid, combine the blueberries, sweetener, water, lemon juice, and butter, and simmer gently. Spoon rounded tablespoons of the biscuit dough onto the blueberries, leaving ½″ between spoonfuls. Cover and simmer gently for 15 minutes. Uncover and test for doneness: a wooden toothpick inserted into the biscuits should come out clean. Cook for an additional 5 minutes if necessary. Serve warm with whipped cream.

Cookies

Zucchinis make great cookies! This is good news for gardeners all over. After all, what gardener does not regularly face the problem of too many zucchinis?

During the height of the summer squash season, I like to keep a close watch on my zucchinis, harvesting them when they are ready, even if my refrigerator is already full of squash. When the squash supply begins to get out of hand, I grate the zucchini and stuff the grated squash into freezer bags and freeze. The squash is then ready to be used in cookies, bread, soufflés, frittatas, or whatever else strikes my fancy later in the year. I defrost the zucchini in a colander and squeeze the defrosted zucchini with my hands to be sure to get rid of as much excess water as possible.

The nice thing about adding vegetables to cookies is that it helps keep the cookies moist and fresh longer. And I like to think that I am adding to the nutritional value of my snacks.

Don't forget to store different types of cookies in separate jars. Soft cookies make crisp cookies soggy when they are stored together.

Pumpkin Chocolate Chip Cookies

PREPARATION TIME: 15 MINUTES
BAKING TIME: 15 MINUTES
YIELD: 4 DOZEN COOKIES

½ cup butter at room
   temperature
1¼ cups brown sugar
2 eggs
1½ cups pureed pumpkin
   (page 5)
2½ cups unbleached all-
   purpose flour
4 teaspoons baking powder
½ teaspoon salt
¼ teaspoon ginger
½ teaspoon nutmeg
½ teaspoon cinnamon
½ cup wheat germ
1 cup chocolate chips
1 cup chopped walnuts

Preheat the oven to 400° F.

Cream together the butter and the sugar. Add the eggs and pumpkin puree.

Sift together the flour, baking powder, salt, and spices. Add the wheat germ, chocolate chips, nuts, and pumpkin mixture and stir until well blended. Drop the batter by the teaspoon about 1½" apart onto a greased cookie sheet. Bake for 15 minutes. Immediately transfer the cookies to a cooling rack.

Variation

Winter Squash Chocolate Chip Cookies. Substitute 1½ cups pureed winter squash (page 5) for the pumpkin.

Apple Butter Sandwich Cookies

PREPARATION TIME: 30 MINUTES
BAKING TIME: 10 MINUTES
YIELD: 2 DOZEN COOKIES

½ **cup butter**
1 **cup unbleached all-purpose flour**
½ **pound cream cheese at room temperature**
⅓ **cup Apple Butter (page 149)**
¾ **teaspoon cinnamon**
2 **tablespoons apple cider**
1 **cup confectioners' sugar**

Preheat the oven to 450° F.

Place the flour in a medium-size mixing bowl and cut in the butter until the texture resembles peas. Add half the cream cheese and mix to make a smooth dough. On a lightly floured board, roll out the dough to a ¼″ thickness. Cut out 1½″ round cookie shapes with a cookie cutter or a glass or empty soupcan dipped in flour. Bake the cookies for 10 minutes or until golden brown. Transfer the cookies to a cooling rack.

Cream together the remaining cream cheese and the apple butter. To make the cider glaze, combine the cinnamon, cider, and confectioners' sugar. Blend until smooth. Add more confectioners' sugar if necessary to thicken the glaze.

When the cookies have cooled, spread the cream cheese and apple butter on one cookie and place another cookie on top to make a sandwich. Spread the cider glaze on the top of the cookies and place in the refrigerator for 30 minutes to harden the filling.

Variation

Pear Butter Sandwich Cookies. Substitute ⅓ cup Pear Butter (page 149) for the Apple Butter.

Zucchini Chocolate Crinkles

PREPARATION TIME: 20 MINUTES
BAKING TIME: 15 MINUTES
YIELD: 4 DOZEN COOKIES

4 ounces unsweetened
  chocolate
½ cup butter
2 cups sugar
1 teaspoon vanilla extract
4 eggs
1 cup grated raw zucchini
2½ cups unbleached all-
  purpose flour
2 teaspoons baking powder
½ teaspoon salt
1 cup chocolate chips
2 cups chopped pecans

In the top of a double boiler, melt the chocolate and butter together. Transfer the chocolate to a mixing bowl and stir in the sugar, vanilla, eggs, and zucchini. Mix well to blend.

Sift together the flour, baking powder, and salt. Stir the dry ingredients into the chocolate mixture until completely blended. Add the chocolate chips and mix well. Chill the batter until firm (at least 4 hours or overnight).

When you are ready to bake the cookies, preheat the oven to 375° F. Form the batter into walnut-sized balls and roll the cookies in the chopped nuts. Place the cookies 2" apart on a greased cookie sheet. Bake for 15 minutes. The cookies will be soft. Cool the cookies on racks.

Variation

Carrot Chocolate Crinkles. Substitute 1 cup grated raw carrots for the zucchini.

Zucchini Coconut Bars

PREPARATION TIME: 30 MINUTES
BAKING TIME: 45 MINUTES
YIELD: 2 DOZEN BARS

Cookie Layer:

½ cup butter at room
    temperature
½ cup sugar
1 cup unbleached all-
    purpose flour

Topping:

2 eggs
1 cup grated raw zucchini
1½ cups brown sugar,
    firmly packed
1 cup shredded coconut
1 cup slivered almonds
1 teaspoon almond extract
2 tablespoons unbleached
    all-purpose flour
½ teaspoon baking powder
dash salt

Preheat the oven to 400° F.

To make the cookie layer, cream together the butter and sugar. Add 1 cup of flour and mix until the dough comes together. Transfer the dough to a greased 9″ × 13″ pan and pat it down to cover the bottom of the pan. Bake the cookie layer for 15 minutes.

In the meantime, beat the eggs, and add the zucchini, brown sugar, coconut, almonds, and almond extract. Mix together the remaining flour, the baking powder, and salt. Add these dry ingredients to the zucchini mixture and blend well.

When the cookie layer is done, spread the zucchini mixture evenly on top. Place the cookies in the oven and bake for 30 minutes. Cool the cookies completely before cutting.

Variations

Green Tomato Coconut Almond Bars. Substitute 2 cups of finely chopped green tomatoes and 1 teaspoon cinnamon for the grated zucchini.

Carrot Coconut Almond Bars. Substitute 1 cup grated raw carrots for the zucchini.

Zuccaroons

PREPARATION TIME: 10 MINUTES
BAKING TIME: 12–15 MINUTES
YIELD: 3–4 DOZEN COOKIES

1 cup grated raw zucchini
1¾ cups bread crumbs
¼ cup unbleached all-
  purpose flour
2 cups finely chopped
  almonds
1 cup white sugar
½ cup brown sugar, firmly
  packed
4 eggs
½ teaspoon almond extract

You can use frozen zucchini in this recipe. Be sure to squeeze the excess moisture out of the zucchini before measuring.

Preheat the oven to 350° F. Mix together all of the ingredients. The mixture will be quite crumbly. Lightly grease a cookie sheet. Place walnut-size pieces of batter 1″ apart on the sheet. Bake on the middle rack of the oven for 12–15 minutes.

Variation
Carrotoons. Substitute 1 cup grated raw carrots for the zucchini.

Eggplant Oatmeal Squares

PREPARATION TIME: 20 MINUTES
BAKING TIME: 35 MINUTES
YIELD: 2 DOZEN SQUARES

Filling:

4 cups eggplant, peeled and
  finely diced
½ cup water
2 tablespoons lemon juice
½ cup brown sugar
½ cup chopped nuts
½ cup chopped dates

Preheat the oven to 350° F.
In a medium-size saucepan, combine the eggplant and water and simmer on medium heat for 5–10 minutes, or until the eggplant is softened. Mix in the lemon juice, ½ cup brown sugar, nuts, and dates. Continue cooking the mixture for 5 minutes, stirring occasionally.

Crust:

2½ cups rolled oats

½ cup butter at
    room temperature

½ cup brown sugar

½ cup unbleached all-
    purpose flour

½ teaspoon baking powder

While the eggplant mixture cooks, mix together the oats, butter, the remaining ½ cup brown sugar, flour, and baking powder. Press half of this mixture into a greased 9″ × 13″ pan. Spread the eggplant mixture evenly over the crust, and sprinkle the remaining oatmeal mixture over the top. Bake at 350° F. for 35 minutes. Cool before cutting into squares.

Peach Walnut Squares

PREPARATION TIME: 20 MINUTES
BAKING TIME: 40 MINUTES
YIELD: 2 DOZEN SQUARES

1 cup whole wheat flour

1½ cups unbleached all-
    purpose flour

½ cup butter

1 cup honey

1 cup walnuts, finely
    ground

1 teaspoon cinnamon

1 teaspoon baking soda

¼ teaspoon salt

1 egg

1 cup yogurt

1 teaspoon vanilla extract

2 cups peeled and finely
    chopped peaches

Preheat the oven to 350° F.

In a medium-size mixing bowl, combine the flours and cut in the butter until the mixture resembles coarse sand. Add the honey and mix well. Stir in the nuts.

Grease a 9″ × 13″ pan. Press 2 cups of the flour and honey mixture into the bottom of the pan. Mix the remaining dough with the rest of the ingredients. Spoon this batter over the crust. Bake for 40 minutes. Cool completely before cutting into squares.

Carrot Chocolate Chip Bars

PREPARATION TIME: 20 MINUTES
BAKING TIME: 40 MINUTES
YIELD: 2 DOZEN COOKIES

½ cup crunchy peanut
  butter
¾ cup sugar
½ cup firmly packed brown
  sugar
2 eggs
1 teaspoon vanilla extract
1¾ cups unbleached all-
  purpose flour
2 teaspoons baking powder
1 teaspoon baking soda
1½ cups grated raw carrots
1 cup chocolate chips

Preheat the oven to 350° F.

Cream together the peanut butter, sugars, eggs, and vanilla. Sift together the flour, baking powder, and baking soda. Mix well with the peanut butter mixture. Stir in the carrots and the chocolate chips. Butter a 9" × 13" pan. Spread the batter evenly in the pan. Bake for 40 minutes, cool completely, and cut in squares.

Sauces, Mincemeats, and Butters

The sauces, mincemeats, and butters in this chapter are used throughout the book.

Take a second look at the sauces. They stand on their own as delicious toppings for fresh and cooked fruits, ice creams, plain pound cakes, gingerbreads—you can probably find dozens of uses for them. And the butters are delicious on toast and ice cream, too.

Basic Soft Custard Sauce

PREPARATION TIME: 5 MINUTES
COOKING TIME: 15 MINUTES
YIELD: 3½ CUPS

3 cups milk
5 egg yolks
2 tablespoons unbleached all-purpose flour
⅓ cup white or brown sugar
1 tablespoon cornstarch
1 teaspoon vanilla extract

Custard sauces are wonderful served over sliced, fresh fruits, or stewed or baked fruits. Custard sauces may be served hot or cold.

Scald the milk in the top of a double boiler that is above, but not in, boiling water.

Mix together the egg yolks, flour, sugar, and cornstarch. Pour in a little of the milk to temper the eggs; then pour the egg mixture into the milk. Continue cooking, stirring constantly until the custard has thickened and coats the spoon. Remove the custard from the heat and strain it through a fine sieve into a chilled bowl. Add the vanilla and serve immediately or chill to serve cold.

Variations

Grand Marnier Sauce. Add 3 tablespoons of Grand Marnier for an elegant sauce for fruit.

Almond Custard. Substitute 1 teaspoon almond extract for the vanilla. Serve over fruit with ground almonds or almond slices.

Sherry Custard. Add ¼ cup sweet cream sherry to the sauce.

Strawberry Zinger Sauce

PREPARATION TIME: 10 MINUTES
YIELD: 1½ CUPS

Serve this sauce over ice cream, melon balls, or sliced peaches or pears.

1½ cups strawberries
3 tablespoons whipping
   cream
1 tablespoon Grand
   Marnier
1 tablespoon Madeira
1 teaspoon lemon juice
2 tablespoons sugar
8 grinds fresh pepper
   (⅛ teaspoon)

Place all the ingredients in a blender or food processor and blend until smooth.

Plum Sauce

PREPARATION TIME: 45 MINUTES
YIELD: 2 CUPS

Plum Sauce goes well with ice cream and poured over Baked Peaches (page 26), Baked Apples (page 25), or Steamed Plum Pudding (page 42).

1 cup dry red wine
1 tablespoon lemon juice
½ cup honey or sugar
1 cinnamon stick
4 whole cloves
4 allspice berries
2 pounds plums, quartered
   and pitted (30 prune
   plums or 8 large plums)

In a medium-size saucepan, combine the wine, lemon juice, and honey, and simmer for 5 minutes. Tie the spices in a cheesecloth bag and put the bag into the pot. Add the plums to the sauce. Cook for 30 minutes or until the plums are very soft. Remove the cheesecloth spice bag and puree the mixture in a blender.

Sour Cherry Sauce

PREPARATION TIME: 15 MINUTES
YIELD: 2½ CUPS

1½ cups sour cherries,
  pitted
1 cup cherry juice or water
1½ tablespoons cornstarch
3 tablespoons honey or
  to taste
½ teaspoon almond extract
juice of 1 lemon

Serve this sauce warm over ice cream, Cherry Sour Cream Honey Cake (page 57), or custard, or use cold as a cheesecake topping.

Combine all the ingredients in a medium-size saucepan. Heat over medium heat until the mixture thickens.

Blueberry Orange Sauce

PREPARATION TIME: 15 MINUTES
YIELD: 2 CUPS

1 cup orange juice
¼ cup honey or sugar
1½ tablespoons flour
1 cup blueberries
2 tablespoons butter

Warmed, this sauce is excellent over ice cream or crepes, or serve it cold as a cheesecake topping or poured over fresh fruit.

In a small saucepan, combine the orange juice and honey, and heat over medium heat until the honey is melted. Put the flour in a small bowl, spoon in some of the orange juice and stir with a fork or whisk until a smooth paste forms. Add a little more juice and blend in, making sure to press out any lumps. Pour the flour mixture back into the pot and add the blueberries. Cook on medium heat for 5 minutes, remove from the heat, and stir in the butter. Serve warm.

Gingered Pear Sauce

PREPARATION TIME: 15 MINUTES
YIELD: 2½ CUPS

Serve warm over Pear Gingerbread Upside-Down Cake (page 60), ice cream, steamed puddings (pages 42 and 44), or gingerbread.

4 pears, peeled and diced
½ cup water plus
    2 tablespoons
¾ cup orange juice
¼ cup brown sugar
1 teaspoon grated lemon
    rind
1 tablespoon lemon juice
2 tablespoons candied ginger
1 tablespoon cornstarch

In a medium-size saucepan, combine the pears, ½ cup water, orange juice, brown sugar, lemon rind, and lemon juice and heat over medium heat.

Place the candied ginger in a blender and spoon in ½ cup of the pear mixture. Blend until smooth and pour back into the pan. Cook for 10 minutes.

While the sauce cooks, mix together the cornstarch and the remaining 2 tablespoons water until there are no lumps. Pour the cornstarch mixture into the pear sauce and cook until thickened.

Lemon Curd

PREPARATION TIME: 10 MINUTES
COOKING TIME: 8–10 MINUTES
YIELD: 1½ CUPS

Lemon Curd is delicious poured over Baked Apples (page 25), Baked Peaches (page 26), Steamed Pumpkin Pudding (page 44), Steamed Plum Pudding (page 42), and sautéed fruits. A very versatile sauce.

2 lemons
1 cup sugar
3 eggs
½ cup butter

Grate the rind of both lemons and place it in a small bowl. Squeeze the juice from the lemons and combine with the lemon rind, sugar, eggs, and butter. Whisk until smooth. Cook the sauce in the top of a double boiler until the sauce thickens, about 8 minutes. Cool and serve over fruit.

Lemon Caramel Sauce

PREPARATION TIME: 10 MINUTES
YIELD: 1 CUP

This sauce can be served over baked apples, peaches, or pears. Or use it as a fondue sauce with strawberries.

¾ cup sugar
3 tablespoons water
1 tablespoon lemon juice
3 tablespoons butter

In a medium-size, heavy-bottomed saucepan, combine the sugar and the water. Heat until the sugar dissolves and the mixture begins to boil. Add the lemon juice and continue boiling the mixture without stirring until the sauce turns a delicate golden brown. Remove the pan from the heat and add the butter. Stir until the butter is melted.

Cider Sauce

PREPARATION TIME: 15 MINUTES
COOKING TIME: 10 MINUTES
YIELD: 2 CUPS

This sauce can be served warm with Steamed Pumpkin Pudding (page 44) or over gingerbread with stewed apples or pears.

2 cups apple cider
2 tablespoons cornstarch
3 allspice berries
6 whole cloves
1 cinnamon stick
1 small piece fresh ginger, peeled
¼ cup honey or brown sugar
1 tablespoon lemon juice

Combine all the ingredients in a medium-size saucepan and cook gently for 10 minutes. Strain out the spices.
Keep the sauce warm in a double boiler until you are ready to serve it.

Chocolate Fondue

PREPARATION TIME: 15 MINUTES
YIELD: 6–8 SERVINGS

12 ounces semisweet
   chocolate
1 cup heavy cream or milk
¼ cup butter
1 tablespoon instant coffee
   powder
2 tablespoons water
2 quarts prepared fruits
   (whole berries, sliced
   apples, peaches, pears)

Place the chocolate, cream, and butter in the top of a double boiler that is over, but not in, boiling water. Stir the coffee into the water and add it to the pot. Heat until the chocolate is melted, stirring often to make a smooth sauce. Transfer the sauce to a chafing dish and serve with the fruit.

Green Tomato Mincemeat

PREPARATION TIME: 30 MINUTES
COOKING TIME: 2 HOURS
YIELD: 10 PINTS

8 cups green tomatoes,
   finely chopped
1–1½ cups cider
   (approximately)
8 cups unpeeled apples,
   finely chopped
1½ pounds raisins
1 pound dates, chopped
2 cups honey
1⅓ cups cider vinegar
2 tablespoons cinnamon
1 teaspoon allspice
2 teaspoons cloves
¼ teaspoon pepper
2 tablespoons grated orange
   rind
⅔ cup vegetable oil

This recipe first appeared in Garden Way's Red and Green Tomato Cookbook.

Drain the chopped green tomatoes for 5–10 minutes, and replace the juice with the same amount of apple cider. Mix all the ingredients, except the oil, in a large stainless steel pot. Simmer until thick—approximately 2 hours. Add the oil and stir well.

If you want to keep the mincemeat for a long time, ladle the hot mincemeat into sterilized, hot pint jars, leaving ½" head space. Seal and process for 25 minutes in a boiling water bath. Complete seals if necessary. You can freeze mincemeat instead of canning, if you wish.

Pear Mincemeat

PREPARATION TIME: 30 MINUTES
COOKING TIME: 2 HOURS
YIELD: 2 QUARTS

Pear Mincemeat is called for in a number of recipes throughout this book, including Pear Mincemeat Custard Pie (page 93) and Mincemeat Pumpkin Pie (page 91). You can use this mincemeat in any recipe calling for green tomato mincemeat.

This recipe makes a rather large quantity. Four cups of the mincemeat make a delicious mincemeat pie. The rest can be frozen.

12 Bartlett or Anjou pears, quartered and cored
1 whole orange, seeded
1 whole lemon, seeded
1 cup honey
½ cup currants
½ cup dates
½ cup raisins
¼ cup crystallized ginger, chopped finely
1 teaspoon cinnamon
¼ teaspoon cloves
¼ teaspoon allspice
¼ cup lemon juice

In a food processor or a food mill, coarsely grind the pears, orange, and lemon. Combine all the ingredients in a large stainless steel pot and simmer for 2 hours, stirring occasionally.

Apple Butter

PREPARATION TIME: 20 MINUTES
COOKING TIME: 3½ HOURS
YIELD: 2½ CUPS

Fruit butters are a traditional preserve that makes good use of windfall and less-than-perfect-looking fruits. Although this recipe uses apples, you can make butters from apricots, peaches, crabapples, plums, pears, grapes, and quinces. I developed this recipe to go with the Apple Butter Cheesecake on page 110.

**4 pounds tart apples,
    quartered**
3 cups apple cider
juice from 2 lemons
2 teaspoons cinnamon
½ teaspoon cloves
¼ teaspoon allspice
¼ teaspoon ginger
1¼ cups honey

In a large, heavy-bottomed pot, combine the apples, cider, and lemon juice. Cook for 30 minutes or until the apples are soft. Strain the apples through a food mill or Squeezo strainer to remove the skins, or process in a food processor and then strain out the skins and seeds.

Return the apple mixture to the pot, and add the remaining ingredients. Continue cooking this mixture for 3 hours or until it is very thick. Stir frequently to prevent scorching.

Pear Butter

PREPARATION TIME: 5 MINUTES
COOKING TIME: 1½ HOURS
YIELD: 1½ CUPS

You can use Pear Butter in any recipe that calls for Apple Butter. This recipe makes a small quantity, but it can easily be multiplied to make a larger quantity. Pear Butter will keep in the refrigerator for up to 3 weeks. Freeze any extra.

2 cups pear puree (page 5)
½ teaspoon cinnamon
¼ teaspoon nutmeg
⅛ teaspoon cloves

Combine all the ingredients in a heavy-bottomed saucepan and cook over medium low heat until the mixture reduces by half. The butter should be so thick a spoon can stand up in it.

Appendix 1
High Altitude Baking

The recipes in this book were all developed and tested at around sea level. Cake batters are particularly sensitive to high altitudes. Here are some formulas for adjusting recipes to high altitudes. If these guidelines don't work for you, consult your local extension home economist.

At 3000-foot elevations and higher:

- Underbeat egg whites.
- Raise baking temperatures by 25 degrees.

At 5000-foot elevations and higher:

- Reduce baking powder by ⅛–¼ teaspoon.
- Increase liquid by 2–3 tablespoons per cup liquid called for and decrease sugar by 1–2 tablespoons for each cup called for.
- Raise baking temperature by 25 degrees.

Appendix 2
Decorating With Chocolate

Decorating with chocolate adds a special, glamorous touch to desserts. The decorations are surprisingly easy to make, but the results are impressive. I always enjoy my guests' comments, especially when they can't figure out how I made the decorations. Here's how it's done.

Melt the Chocolate

The first thing to do is melt the chocolate. For these designs you can use semisweet chocolate chips or squares. Make sure your pan is absolutely dry. Melt the chocolate in a double boiler that is over, but not in, boiling water. Be very, very careful not to allow any water to drip into the chocolate.

Make a Piping Bag

You will need a piping bag for the filigrees and the butterfly. Make the bag out of waxed paper or parchment paper. Cut a piece of paper to make a 15–18″ square. Fold the square in half to make a triangle. Roll the triangle into a cone. Tape the cone to hold the shape. Cut off the very tip of the cone, if necessary, to make an opening the size of a pin head.

Spoon the melted chocolate into the cone. Fill the cone half full. Fold over the top to prevent the chocolate from oozing out. With your right hand (if you are right-handed), press gently from the top of the cone while cradling the cone in your left hand. The chocolate will be

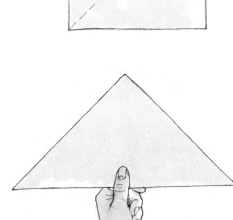
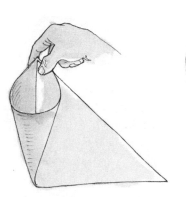

chocolate filigrees

piped out in a smooth line. Practice piping with the chocolate on waxed paper. It is also helpful to trace the designs you want to make on the back of the waxed paper. Then follow the lines you made.

Chocolate Filigrees

These chocolate ornaments can be pressed into the side of cake, stood vertically on top of a cake, or placed on top of a fruit dish. Allow 1 filigree per serving and figure that ½ cup of melted semisweet chocolate will make several filigrees.

Use the designs shown here or invent your own. Trace out the design with melted chocolate piped on waxed paper. Chill thoroughly and peel off the filigrees just before serving.

Chocolate Butterflies

These butterflies can be perched on top of cakes and mousses. Figure that ½ cup of melted semisweet chocolate chips will make 2 butterflies.

Trace the outlines of the butterfly wings and bodies onto a piece of waxed paper, as shown. Fill in the center of the wings with a design of your choice, making sure each chocolate wing line touches the chocolate outline. Fill in the bodies of the butterflies completely. Refrigerate the butterflies until you are ready to use them.

To assemble the butterflies on top of a cake or mousse, peel off the waxed paper. Place a dollop of whipped cream or frosting on the cake. Press the butterfly body into the icing. Spoon a smaller dollop of whipped cream or frosting on each side of the body. Press the wings into the icing at an angle, as though the butterfly was about to take flight.

chocolate butterfly

Chocolate Leaves

Chocolate leaves can be pressed into the sides of a frosted cake or placed on top of a cake, mousse, or fruit dish. Figure that ½ cup of melted semisweet chocolate chips will make about 12 leaves. Make extras because some will crack. I like to use rose leaves, but I imagine any tough-skinned, nonpoisonous leaf will work as well.

Melt the chocolate in a double boiler. Draw a leaf across the top of the chocolate, completely covering the front side of the leaf. Place the leaf, chocolate side up, on a piece of waxed paper. When all the leaves are covered in this fashion, chill at least 15 minutes, or until you are ready to use them. Peel off the waxed paper, leaving perfect chocolate leaves.

Index